REAL KIDS
REAL ADVENTURES

REAL KIDS REAL ADVENTURES

TRUE STORIES BY DEBORAH MORRIS

ADRIFT IN THE ATLANTIC

BLINDED AT BIG HOLE

BLIZZARD IN WILDCAT HILLS

BROADMAN
& HOLMAN
PUBLISHERS

Nashville, Tennessee

© 1994
Broadman & Holman Publishers
All rights reserved

Printed in the United States of America

4240-52
0-8054-4052-6

Dewey Decimal Classification: JSC
Subject Heading: Courage—Nonfiction // Faith—Nonfiction
Library of Congress Card Catalog Number: 94-11741

Library of Congress Cataloging-in-Publication Data
Morris, Deborah, 1956–
    Real kids, real adventures / by Deborah Morris.
        p.   cm.
    ISBN 0-8054-4051-8
    1. Christian biography—United States—Juvenile literature.
2. Children—United States—Biography—Juvenile literature.
[1. Survival. 2. Adventure and adventurers.   3. Christian
biography.]   I. Title.
BR1714.M67   1994
209'.2'273—dc20   94-11741
[B]   CIP
                                                         AC

ISBN 0-8054-4051-8 (vol. 1)
ISBN 0-8054-4052-6 (vol. 2)

To Lisa, Rachel, Steven, and Sean,
my own wild adventurers.

Matthew Sperber (r), his father Michael (l), and J. B.
Stephens after their rescue from the Atlantic Ocean.
Photo courtesy of the *Sun-Sentinel*

Adrift in the Atlantic

The Matthew Sperber Story

Matthew slowly opened one eye and then lifted his
head from his pillow just far enough to see the clock
on his dresser. The harsh Florida sunlight streaming
in through the window made his eyes hurt as he
squinted to read the clock's dim, red numbers. It was
11:06 A.M.

Burying his face back into his pillow for another
moment, Matthew finally rolled over and sat up. He
stretched, waving his arms in the air. *Summertime,* he

1

thought, yawning, *is made for sleeping.* He slowly pulled himself out of bed. Too bad there were only five more weeks left. Soon it would be back to the grind attending tenth grade at Forest Hill High.

Walking through the TV room on his way to the kitchen, he grunted a greeting to his little brother, Adam. Adam, who was watching cartoons, didn't look up. Matthew poured himself a huge bowl of Apple Jacks and then took it over to the bar where he could see the TV. Adam was watching a re-re-rerun of an old "Road Runner" cartoon.

Matthew shoveled a spoonful of Apple Jacks™ into his mouth and mumbled around them, "Hey, can't you find a different cartoon? You've seen this one a zillion times."

"No. I like it."

It figures, Matthew thought. He considered changing the channel but decided it wasn't worth it; Adam would throw a fit. He'd planned to go out in the boat right after breakfast anyway. Adam could stay home and watch the Road Runner™ and Wiley Coyote™ till his eyes fell out.

He finished his cereal and went to his room to get dressed. The slice of sky he could see through the mini-blinds looked bright and sunny—a typical July day in West Palm Beach. Going out on the lake would be fun. He loved the sixteen-foot bass boat his parents had given him for Christmas the year before. Even though he'd owned other boats— a small aluminum boat he'd gotten when he was eight, and later a jon boat—the blue bass boat was a dream come true. It wasn't as fancy as his father's big fishing boat, but it was just right for cruising around with friends.

Pulling on a pair of cut-offs and a Tee-shirt, the fourteen-year-old walked over to his bedroom shelves lined with Little League trophies and baseball caps. He stuck his favorite Billabong surf cap on over his dark, rumpled hair and hesitated, looking at his equally rumpled bed. But after all, he reasoned, it *was* summertime. Why make the bed when he'd be sleeping in it again tonight?

Betty Sperber was in the kitchen loading the bowls and cups from breakfast into the dishwasher. A nurse at St. Mary's Hospital, Mrs. Sperber took most summers off so she could be at home with Matthew and Adam. She was slender and pretty with long dark hair, but she was kind of a neat freak around the house. She hated seeing dishes standing in the sink.

When Matthew walked in, she looked up and smiled. "Heading out?"

"Yeah. I'm going fishing, probably with Bobby." Stepping up behind her, Matthew put his hands on her shoulders and leaned against her back to give her a half-hug. Mrs. Sperber staggered under his weight. He was already bigger than she was.

"Hey!" she laughed, giving him an affectionate pat on the cheek. "You're about to knock me down!"

"Maybe if you ate more you'd be strong like me."

"Right. Well, you and Bobby have lots of fun. Just make sure you're back by dark. And you guys watch your speed out on the lake, you hear me? I don't want any racing around."

"All right. See you!"

Matthew passed through the living room, glancing up at the long needle-nose of the blue-and-silver sailfish mounted on the wall. His dad had caught it out at the pier at age thirteen. Matthew was still waiting to land his first sailfish. He was already a year behind in following in his father's "fabled" fishing footsteps.

Stepping out onto the front porch, he grabbed his skateboard out of the bushes and rode it smoothly down to the sidewalk. His boat was docked at his grandparents' house a few streets away. He skated to the end of the block and turned right at the stop sign. When he rolled into his grandparents' driveway a few minutes later he tried to be quiet, not wanting to attract their attention. He wasn't in the mood today to stop and talk.

Tucking his skateboard under his arm, he eased through the gate in the chain-link fence, and then cut around to the back yard. The house was situated right on a canal. His boat, a sleek, blue craft with four plastic seats, was tied up by the seawall. He jumped down lightly onto the gray-carpeted deck and then snapped his fishing pole into the plastic hooks neatly lining the side. Time for some serious fishing!

After casting off the bowline and starting the motor, he "putted" down the canal. His friend Bobby lived just around the corner, also on the water.

Five minutes later he floated to a stop behind Bobby's ski boat. "Hey!" he yelled, standing up and waving toward the house. "Bobby! Come on out!"

The sliding glass door opened and a heavyset boy with dark hair stepped out. Bobby was two years older but about the same height as Matthew. He ran down to the seawall.

"Hi," he said breathlessly. "You want to take my boat, too, or just go in yours?"

"I don't care. Why don't we just go in mine for now? I want to do some fishing."

"Okay. I'll be right back." Bobby ran back into his house. When he reappeared he was carrying a fishing pole in one hand and a BB rifle in the other.

He jumped down into the boat with Matthew. "I'm taking my rifle along in case we fish under the bridge," he explained. "I'm not crazy about having all those dirty pigeons sitting right over my head like that."

Matthew grinned. "Do you think you'll be able to hit anything with that?"

"Probably. Enough to scare them off, anyway."

Matthew eased the boat down the canal until they reached the point where it spilled into Lake Clarke. Finally, a chance to get up some speed! He shoved the throttle forward, enjoying the feeling of power as the boat surged ahead.

"So," he yelled as they bounced and skipped over the small waves, "what've you been up to?"

"Not much," Bobby yelled back. "Just sitting around the house mostly. What about you?"

"Same thing. My dad made me work all day last Saturday at his jewelry store, so that really stunk. I told him I didn't want to, but he wouldn't listen. He always does that to me." He shrugged. "But at least now I have some money to spend. We can grab some burgers at McDonald's™ later."

He turned the wheel slightly, heading toward a spot in the lake where he'd caught several bass the last time he was out. When he got close to the spot he eased back on the throttle and let the boat sort of drift in that direction. He finally switched off the motor. *Better not scare the fish,* he decided.

Bobby was already reaching for his fishing pole. "When are you and your dad leaving for the Bahamas? Is it next week or the week after?"

"Next week, on Wednesday. I can't wait. We're going to Walker's Cay this time. Dad's friend, J. B., is going along, too, and he has a boat down there we can use the whole time. It'll be great."

Matthew cast his favorite black-and-gold Rapala lure out across the water. He smiled with confidence when he saw it drop neatly in the middle of a fishy-looking spot. He let it sink for a few seconds before starting slowly to reel it back in. *Come on, bass,* he said silently. *Bite that delicious-looking lure.*

"Did you mention to your dad that you have this really good friend who'd like to go along?" Bobby asked teasingly, casting his line several feet away. "You guys might need somebody to help carry your fishing poles and stuff, you know."

"Sorry. Dad's not even taking Adam. He says he whines too much."

"Got that right. Are you guys flying there or going by boat?"

"Walking," Matthew quipped. "No, really, we're flying this time. Dad and J. B. are chartering a little plane to take us there."

"Lucky! How long are you going to be gone?"

"Five days. Five whole days of fishing and snorkeling in the Bahamas. Ahhh."

Bobby shook his head in disgust. "I ought to throw you overboard. I've never been to the Bahamas even once and you're on your fourth or fifth trip. It's not fair."

"Aw, poor baby," Matthew said, grinning. "I'll think of you while I'm catching all those fish. Those *big* fish."

"I bet."

The two fell quiet for a while, concentrating on their fishing. After fifteen minutes of casting and reeling in, Matthew felt a sharp tug on his line. He jerked the tip of his rod up just enough to set the hook.

"Got it!" he crowed, as he felt the solid weight of the fish pulling against his line. "Feels like a big one, too."

Bobby was busy reeling in his lure. "What is it?"

"Feels like a bass. It's fighting like crazy." Matthew skillfully eased the fish closer and closer to the boat, letting it wear itself out. Finally, when it splashed to the surface just a few feet away, they both saw the yellow-green color and dark band along the side—definitely a largemouth bass.

"Here, hand me the net," Matthew said, waving his hand at Bobby. He pulled the fish a little closer, and scooped it up and into the boat. Hooking his fingers into its gills, he held it up.

"Pretty one," Bobby admitted. "Looks like about a three-pounder."

"Yep." Matthew started working to unhook the lure from its mouth. "I'm not going to keep it, though. I don't feel like cleaning it."

After carefully removing the lure, Matthew paused long enough to give the flapping fish one last admiring glance, then gently lowered it back into the water. The fish hovered near the surface for just a moment, confused, before disappearing downward with one sharp flip of its tail.

Over the next two hours Bobby caught one bass and a catfish. Matthew didn't catch anything. At around two o'clock they both decided to go get some burgers from the McDonald's nearby. Their hands smelled a little fishy as they ate but they didn't care. It wasn't worth washing up when they were going right back out to fish some more.

After lunch they headed for the bridge. They saw that the pigeons were everywhere, flapping back and forth between the nests they'd built. The steel beams overhead were covered with white pigeon droppings.

"Stupid birds," Bobby muttered, reaching for his BB rifle. "You're not going to get me this time!" Matthew stopped the boat away from bridge. Bobby lifted his rifle and took aim at a particularly loud pigeon that looked as if it was waiting to bomb them. Right as he pulled the trigger, though, the bird took off. The BB pinged harmlessly against the steel.

"Missed!" Matthew said. "Why don't you try for that fat one over there?"

Bobby nodded, pumping up his rifle again. This time when he pulled the trigger, the pigeon squawked and fluttered off. Bullseye!

After scaring five or six of them off, Bobby reached for his fishing pole. Time to get down to business. There were fish waiting to be caught!

Sibling Rivalry

It was almost seven o'clock before Matthew got back home that night. His dad had just come in from work at the jewelry store he owned, and he was settled in his recliner watching the news.

"Hi, Dad," Matthew said.

"Hi, son" Mike Sperber replied. "How was fishing today?"

"Fine. I got a couple bass. Nice ones, too."

"Sounds great. Good practice for next week!"

Matthew laughed. "Yeah. Bobby's jealous. He asked if he could go along with us to help carry our fishing poles and stuff when we go to the Bahamas."

His dad smiled. "I don't think so. Nice try though."

After a shower and dinner, Matthew felt lazy. Being in the sun all day left him feeling drained. Maybe he'd just watch TV for a while and go to bed. But when Adam trooped through the room with three of his friends, heading for the pool in the backyard, Matthew woke up a little. It might be fun to play a game of Marco Polo.

A few minutes later, splashing in the pool, he grinned as his little brother yelled, "Marco!" from just two feet away. He waited until Eric and Wesley distracted Adam by answering, "Polo!" from the other side of the pool before chiming in; then he dove down to shoot across the pool underwater. By the time Adam whirled around, arms outstretched, he was long gone.

They played for over an hour, laughing and dunking each other between games. But when Adam lost his second game in a row, he got upset. He swam over and shoved Matthew angrily.

"You wouldn't have caught me if Eric hadn't been in my way," he said. "It's not fair."

Most of the time Matthew let things go rather than fight about them. But he didn't like being shoved, especially by Adam, the little creep.

"Don't shove me," he said firmly. Turning his back, he started up the steps to get out of the pool— but he gasped as a hard fist caught him between the shoulder blades. He whirled around to face his little brother.

"Knock it off, Adam!" he shouted. "What are you, stupid? I'm twice your size!"

"I don't care! Come on. I dare you!"

Matthew was tempted—*really* tempted—to teach Adam a lesson, but he knew what would happen if he hauled off and hit him. Besides, even though his brother was a pain, he didn't really want to hurt him bad.

"Why don't you just grow up?" he said. "You know you're just going to get into trouble if Mom and Dad find out. Go play with your little friends."

Matthew started toward the house. Adam took another half-hearted swing at him, but Matthew just kept going. What was Adam's problem, anyway? Did he *want* to get beat up?

Mrs. Sperber was just walking out of the kitchen. "What was going on out there? I thought I heard some yelling."

"It was Adam. He got mad because he lost a game."

She shook her head. "Eleven sure seems to be a rough age for him. I don't remember your being this edgy."

Matthew shrugged. "You can't have *all* perfect kids, you know. One to a family. And you've already got me." Mrs. Sperber laughed.

The next week seemed to fly by. On Tuesday night Matthew and Mr. Sperber stayed up late packing their bags and gathering up all their fishing and diving gear for their trip early the next morning.

"Matthew, go put this stuff out in my truck," Mr. Sperber said, holding out a plastic bag filled with their snorkels, masks, and diving fins. "Then come back in and get the big, red cooler."

Matthew was busy organizing his tackle box, but he stood up without a word. Mr. Sperber, an ex-navy man, expected to be obeyed without a lot of back talk. Matthew had learned a long time ago to keep his mouth shut and do what he was told.

Off to the Bahamas

They rose early the next morning to leave for the airport. J. B. was supposed to meet them there. J. B. Stephens, a long-time friend of Mr. Sperber's, was a big, hearty man in his early fifties. Matthew didn't know him very well, but he seemed pretty nice. He looked a little like Skipper on "Gilligan's Island."

At Palm Beach International Airport, Mr. Sperber drove around to the Biz-Jet Executive Terminal where Palm Beach Aviation, the company they had hired to fly them to the Bahamas, was located. J. B. pulled up at the same time. The pilot of the Cherokee Six single-engine plane they'd be flying in was waiting. He was a tall man with a friendly smile.

"Hi, folks!" he called warmly. "You must be the ones heading for Walker's Cay this morning. My name's Don and I'll be your pilot."

J. B. stuck out his hand. "I'm Joe Stephens," he said, "and this is Mike Sperber and his son, Matthew."

"Nice to meet you," Don said, shaking hands all around. "Let me help you load all your stuff and then we can be on our way."

After Matthew helped carry some of the gear from his dad's truck over to the plane, he watched as the pilot shoved it all inside the small baggage compartment beneath the plane's belly.

"You can go ahead and board now," Don said. "Just watch your heads."

When Matthew climbed in, he was surprised at how small the plane was. Besides the pilot and copilot's seats, there were only two other seats in the back. He slid into one of the back seats, and J. B. settled into the seat beside him. Mike Sperber sat up front in the copilot's seat.

Don climbed in and closed the door. "All right," he said. "Before we get started, let me point out a few things. You've all got seat belts, and you need to put them on and keep them on. This will only be about a forty-five-minute flight so it shouldn't be too uncomfortable."

Matthew felt for his seat belt. This was really going to be fun. He was only half-listening as the pilot told them where their lifejackets were stowed and explained what to do if the plane had to "ditch" over water. He sounded as if he'd given the same speech a million times before.

Matthew let his mind drift to the exciting days ahead. Maybe, he thought, he'd get lucky and catch his sailfish this trip. If he did, he wouldn't bring it home to stuff; there weren't that many sailfish left in the ocean anymore. He'd just take a quick picture and let it go.

He snapped back to attention when the engine roared to life. A few minutes later they rolled down the runway and soared into the air. They were on their way!

As they headed out over the ocean, Matthew relaxed in his seat, and stared down at the blue waves sparkling below. It looked neat to see the Florida coast from the air like this. The other times he and his dad had gone down to the Bahamas they'd traveled by boat. It had taken them almost three hours to get there.

This time, the trip was over almost before they knew it. The tiny airstrip on Walker's Cay was perched on the edge of a coral cliff. Matthew looked doubtfully at the short, uneven runway. He wondered if they didn't stop in time, if they might not splash right into the water!

But Don landed the Cherokee Six without trouble and came to a bumpy halt well before reaching the end of the runway.

"Well, here we are!" he said cheerfully as they taxied back toward the low white building where the Customs and Immigrations officials waited. "I'll help you carry your luggage inside, but then I have to take off again. I hope you folks have a good vacation here on the island."

"I'm sure we will," Mr. Sperber said. "Thanks."

It was a few minutes after nine o'clock when they all walked inside. Matthew waited impatiently as his father and J. B. filled out a bunch of papers and let the Customs Inspectors inspect all their luggage. He passed the time by reading the "Warning" posters plastered all over the walls, telling all the things you weren't allowed to bring onto the island. *Good thing,* he thought, *that we aren't trying to smuggle in guns or drugs.* Several policemen were standing around looking bored. They'd probably love some action.

By ten o'clock they were ready to leave. J. B.'s boat, a big twenty-four foot open fisherman with a tall observation tower, was docked at the Walker's Cay Marina, right next to the airport. They lugged their gear over to the marina and soon were climbing into the boat.

"Rosie's is about twenty minutes away," J. B. said. Rosie's was the waterfront hotel where they'd be staying. "Just settle back and enjoy yourselves!"

"Sounds good to me," Mr. Sperber said, plopping down in a deck chair. The sky was bright blue and sunny, the breeze off the water pleasant. Matthew sat near the rail. As J. B. navigated the boat around the island, Matthew stared at the small, brightly-colored houses visible along the shoreline and through the trees. They looked different from houses in the United States, more casual and open.

"Matthew, did you know that there isn't a single car on the whole island?" J. B. asked. "The closest thing to a car here is the golf cart that the local minister drives. It's a whole different way of life than we're used to."

Matthew laughed. "Sounds neat."

When they reached Rosie's Hotel and Marina, Matthew examined the area with interest. It was a rustic two- story building with several small balconies overlooking the marina and dock. J. B. would be able to dock his boat there the whole time.

They checked in and went up to the room they'd all be sharing on the second floor. It was small but clean, with an ice-cold air conditioner. Matthew quickly dumped his bag on one of the beds so he could step outside onto the balcony. He drew a deep breath of the warm, moist air, tinged with the sea-scents of salt and seaweed. *This is going to be great!* he decided.

Over the days that followed, the three settled into a comfortable routine. They'd get up at around eight o'clock each morning, go downstairs to eat breakfast, and then head out in J. B.'s boat to fish or snorkel all day. After several days of "free-diving"—diving without oxygen tanks—they could all hold their breaths for a long time. Arriving back at the hotel each night, they'd eat dinner and stay up listening to music until bedtime. Matthew loved every minute of it.

The only bad thing was that he thought his father, as usual, was treating him like slave labor. "Clean the boat." "Bring me a Coke.™" "Carry this." "Do that." Matthew wished he could talk to him sometimes about what was really on his mind, but he was afraid to. His dad probably wouldn't understand. Parents almost never did.

By the last afternoon, they had caught enough fish to fill three big coolers. Matthew hadn't landed a sailfish but had caught plenty of snapper, grouper, and even dove for lobster. He was sunburned but happy.

"I'm not ready to go home yet," he sighed as they headed back to the hotel for the last time. "Can't we stay another couple days?"

"Afraid not," his dad said. He rubbed the dark, stubbly beard on his chin. Neither he nor J. B. had shaved since they'd left Florida. "I've got to get back to work. I don't have a whole summer off like you, you know."

Matthew was tempted to say, *I'm not exactly "off" when I have to spend almost every Saturday at Michael's Jewelers,* but he bit his tongue. "Yeah," he mumbled.

Pulling up to the dock at Rosie's, they all climbed out and went upstairs to get cleaned up for the trip home. They were supposed to be back at the Walker's Cay Airport at four o'clock.

As Matthew waited his turn for the shower, he laid back on the bed, feeling a little itchy from the salt air. His mom was going to be surprised when she saw how much fish they were bringing home. Even after they divided it up with J. B. there'd be enough to last a year.

By the time they all showered, changed clothes, and repacked their gear, they were running almost an hour late in getting to the airport. This time a different plane was waiting to take them home, a twin-engine Aero Commander 500. The pilot, Jerry Langford, was an older man, skinny as a rail and wearing glasses. Now, when compared to their dark suntans, Matthew thought his skin looked dead white.

"Ah, there you are!" he called out as they trudged up. "I was starting to get worried."

"Sorry we're late," J. B. said. "It just took a little longer than we'd expected to get our stuff together. This place is kind of hard to leave."

Mr. Langford nodded. "Well, I guess we'd better get moving. Let me load your baggage."

When Matthew climbed into the plane he saw that this one had two extra seats facing backwards, positioned back-to-back with the pilot's and copilot's seats. He considered sitting in one of them, but he decided he'd rather face forward. He took the farthest-back seat on the right. Like before, J. B. took the seat beside him and Mike Sperber sat up front.

Mr. Langford got in, started the engines, and went through the brief pre-flight check. Matthew noticed that this plane had wings above the cabin instead of below. At his right elbow there was a small escape hatch that said in big red letters: "Turn Handle and Pull Toward You."

Not a good idea, Matthew thought humorously as the plane started rolling down the runway, *if you're up in the air.* He decided to keep his hands off it.

They shot up off the runway like a rock from a slingshot, and within seconds the little plane was climbing out over the clear, blue water. Matthew felt a slight thumping underfoot as the landing gear folded up into the plane's belly.

"Sure is pretty up here, isn't it?" His dad said, raising his voice to carry over the engines. "Matthew, see how the water is a lighter color all around the island where it's shallow? It'll get a little darker as we go farther out, but we'll still be over the 'flats' for a while. The water's only ten- to fifty-feet deep along the flats, but in about twenty minutes the bottom will drop off all of a sudden. If you watch, you'll see a vivid color change as we go over the edge."

"Neat," Matthew shouted back, peering out his window. A few minutes later J. B. nudged him.

"See that?" He pointed down to a large, triangular rock jutting up from the waves. It had a tall pole with a blinking light. "That's Memory Rock. We passed it the other day, remember?"

Matthew nodded. Funny to see how far out they'd gone in the boat. J. B. sighed and leaned back in his seat, half-closing his eyes. Matthew yawned, lulled by the drone of the engines. It would be so easy to fall asleep.

But he didn't want to miss the last few minutes of their trip. He looked back out the window. There were several boats just below inching along across the water. One, a white boat, was probably fairly large. But from four thousand feet up they all looked like little bathtub toys.

They'd been flying for about twenty minutes when Mr. Sperber got Matthew's attention and pointed down. Matthew pressed his face against the window. The ocean below was changing abruptly from a cheerful light blue to almost black. This must be the "edge," where the deep water began. That was where the really big fish lurked—tuna, marlin, sailfish, and of course sharks.

He was still staring down when a loud *bang!* made him jump. The sound of the plane's engines suddenly became much quieter. Matthew watched in alarm as his father leaned sideways in the copilot's seat to look over at the pilot's gauges. Mr. Langford was flipping a number of switches but nothing was happening. Matthew's heart gave a lurch. Something was wrong!

"Dad?" he said. "What's—"

A second loud *bang!* sounded, drowning out his voice. An eerie silence instantly fell inside the small cabin. Matthew gripped the sides of his seat as the plane shuddered and then started dropping.

The pilot flipped a switch on the radio, pre-set to an emergency frequency.

"Mayday! Mayday!" he said. "This is Charlie 40. I have total engine failure! Repeat, total engine failure . . . ."

Matthew's stomach churned. He was too scared to move, too scared to even think.

"Turn back to the right, toward the flats!" His dad told the pilot. "We just passed a boat back there!"

The moment Mr. Langford eased the plane right, however, it faltered—then fell like a rock, the nose tilting down at an alarming angle. "We're going down!" he shouted.

Plane Crash in the Atlantic

J. B. leaned forward. "Do we have a life raft on board?" he asked quickly. "Or life jackets?"

Mr. Langford was still struggling with the controls. "No life raft . . . the life jackets are under your seat."

J. B. reached down and slid out a gray cardboard box. Inside were five yellow life jackets. He started passing them out.

Mr. Sperber took his, and quickly twisted in his seat to check on Matthew. His eyes immediately fell on the seat belt dangling forgotten from the teenager's seat.

"Matthew, get your seat belt on!" he ordered. "And get that life jacket on! Hurry!"

Matthew nodded in a daze. Snapping his seat belt first he unfolded the plastic life jacket J. B. handed him and slipped it over his head. Shaped like a horse shoe, it was the kind that inflated with a jerk on a little red cord on the side. He vaguely remembered Don, the first pilot, explaining that you shouldn't inflate it till you were out of the plane. He pulled the long nylon strap around his waist and fastened it. Beside him, J. B. did the same thing.

Mr. Langford was still fighting to restart the engines, but it wasn't working. They continued their headlong plunge toward the waves.

"Brace yourselves!" he finally said in a tight voice.

Matthew glanced out the window again in terror. The waves seemed to be rushing up to meet the plane. His seat felt as if it was dropping out from under him, faster and faster like a runaway rollercoaster.

"Matthew!" Mr. Sperber said, twisting around in his seat again. "When we hit the water, don't you wait for anything; just get out as fast as you can. Do you understand?"

"Yes, sir." Matthew felt a hard lump in his throat. The look on his father's face—this wasn't right. They weren't supposed to crash. It wasn't supposed to be like this! His heart pounded against his ribs making it hard for him to breath. He peeked out the window again, but froze. The waves were only a few feet away!

At the last instant, J. B. leaned over and pulled him down, trying to cover him with his own bear-like body. Seconds before the nose of the plane hit the water, Matthew screamed: "Dad, *I love you!*"

/ / /

At home, Mrs. Sperber was busy putting the finishing touches on a homemade chocolate cake. She had spent a peaceful Sunday afternoon relaxing out by the pool before coming in to put a roast in the oven. Adam was playing next door, so the house was quiet. She hummed softly as she smoothed the rich chocolate frosting onto the cake, a welcome-home dessert for her husband and older son. It would be nice to have the whole family back together again!

She expected them to be getting home at around five-thirty, so she had planned dinner for six. After eating at a restaurant all week, she knew they'd probably be more than ready for a good home-cooked meal.

But five-thirty crept by, then six o'clock, with no sign of Mr. Sperber's truck pulling into the driveway. Mrs. Sperber kept glancing at the clock, wondering what was keeping them. If they didn't show up soon, the roast was going to be ruined.

"If those guys are just hanging out at the airport swapping fish stories, I'm going to kill them," she muttered to herself as six-thirty approached. "They could at least call!"

But after another half-hour passed without word, she started getting worried. What if something had happened? When the phone rang, she snatched it up, relieved. Mike and Matthew had probably been delayed on Walker's Cay for some reason. Maybe they'd taken a later flight.

But it was a woman's voice. "Is this Mike's wife?" she asked.

"Yes. Who's this?"

To her dismay, the woman burst into tears. "I'm J. B.'s friend," she sobbed. "I went to the airport to pick him up a while ago, and he wasn't there. The Coast Guard says that their plane went down in the ocean!"

Mrs. Sperber listened in disbelief as the woman told how a fisherman had reported hearing a single mayday call. Then . . . nothing. When Mrs. Sperber hung up a few minutes later her hands were shaking.

She stared down at her hands, unable to fully take in the news. Nightmarish images rose before her eyes: Matthew screaming in fear as the plane went down . . . her husband struggling to escape as the plane sank beneath the waves, trapping him inside. . . .

She moaned and covered her face. "Don't let them be dead," she sobbed. "Please let them be okay!"

Then she remembered Adam. He was still next door playing with friends. She couldn't let him hear this from somebody else. She ran out front and called him. He came bouncing up to her, but he stopped short when he saw her face.

"What's the matter?" he asked, alarmed.

Mrs. Sperber quickly drew him inside the house. She put her arms around him. "Adam," she said, trying to keep her voice steady, "the plane your dad and Matthew were on went down in the ocean."

Adam's eyes widened with shock. "No!" he said, shoving away from her. "No! No! *No!*"

Mrs. Sperber watched helplessly as he burst into hysterical tears, flailing his arms as he stumbled back and forth. She grabbed him again and held him tight.

"The Coast Guard is already out looking for them," she assured him. "They'll probably find them any minute. And Matthew and your dad are both strong swimmers, you know that. They'll be okay."

She continued to talk, trying to soothe Adam's fears. She just wished she could soothe away her own dark thoughts.

Staying Afloat

The plane hit the water with an explosive roar, smacking across the surface like a skipping rock. Matthew was tossed forward as the metal skin of the fuselage ripped apart with a deafening clang, echoing like a giant metal drum hit by a sledge hammer. Water instantly rushed in like a waterfall. By the time the plane stopped, the water was up to Matthew's knees.

Mike Sperber was already out of his seat. "Get the door open!" he yelled. J. B. immediately turned to attack the door, twisting the handle and shoving outward with all his might.

"It's jammed, Mike!" he yelled.

Matthew looked around in terror. The water was now halfway up his chest—and rising fast. They had to get out of here!

Suddenly, he remembered the escape hatch next to his seat. If he could open that, they'd be able to swim out that way! Groping under the water, he found the handle, then turned it and pulled as hard as he could. Nothing happened.

His father was already lunging back through the rising water to help J. B. with the door, walking doubled over to fit under the low ceiling. Matthew tried to stand up, but he had forgotten about his seat belt. It held him pinned in place. With panic rising in his throat, he reached down and clawed at the metal buckle. To his horror, it too was jammed. The water was now up to his neck.

"Dad!" he screamed. "I can't get my seat belt off!"

As J. B. continued to ram his massive shoulder against the now-submerged door, Mike Sperber turned to help Matthew. The pilot was standing beside his seat, looking dazed, holding the back of his head. His life jacket was hanging loose around his neck. Only a small pocket of air now remained near the cabin's ceiling. If they didn't find a way out within seconds they were all going to drown.

Water lapped up over Matthew's chin when Mr. Sperber's desperate effort to free him finally worked. As the seat belt sprang apart, the teenager bobbed up, heart pounding.

At that same moment, J. B. broke down the door. With one mighty heave he shoved it out against the pressing sea, then reached back to grab Matthew. Without hesitation he dove down to swim out, dragging Matthew along with him.

Although it was only about a ten-foot swim from the cabin door to the surface, swimming through the clear blue-grey water seemed to take forever. When Matthew burst up through the water outside, he drew a deep, gasping breath. Air!

J. B. pulled Matthew over to the plane's wing and said, "Hang on!" before starting back toward the door to help the others. Matthew grabbed on, remembering then to pull the red cord on his life jacket. Instantly, the jacket puffed up, inflated by the metal carbon dioxide cartridge built into the front.

Seconds later Mike Sperber popped up in the water next to J. B. "Dad!" Matthew yelled. "Over here!"

Mr. Sperber swam over and gave Matthew's shoulder a comforting squeeze. "You okay, son?"

"Yeah. I can't believe this."

"Me either."

J. B. was just about to dive back into the water to get Mr. Langford out of the plane when the pilot finally surfaced. Splashing awkwardly, he sputtered, "I can't swim!" J. B. grabbed his arm and swam him over to the others, where he could lift the frightened pilot up onto the wing itself.

"Where's your life vest?" J. B. demanded.

The pilot looked down. His glasses were gone and blood was streaming down his face. He looked dazed. "I don't know. It must've gotten ripped off as I swam out." He added numbly, "My head hurts."

Matthew looked at the injured man before turning to his dad. "Should I give him my life jacket?" he asked in a low voice. "I'm a good swimmer."

"No!" Mr. Sperber said sharply. "We'll have to figure out something else for him. You keep that vest on."

One by one, the rest of them climbed up on the wing to sit. It was more comfortable than treading water. J. B. examined the back of the pilot's head. His scalp was gashed in several places, but it wasn't serious. He guessed he might be suffering from a concussion, though.

"So, Mike," J. B. said. "What do you think . . . an hour and a half till they pick us up?"

Mr. Sperber thought. "Takes the Coast Guard about an hour to respond, so it should be about that." He shook his head. "This'll be some story to tell tonight, won't it? Not the way I'd planned to end the trip."

J. B. slid down off the wing. "What do you say we dive down and try to get a couple of our coolers out before the plane sinks? They'll make good floats. I think Jerry's going to need one."

Turning toward the plane, though, he saw that the tail was already starting to dip down in the water. "Forget that idea," he said. "We need to get away from here. It's going down!"

Matthew slipped back into the water. It was warm and flat as glass, still reflecting the hot afternoon sun. He peered down, able to see his legs and tennis shoes clearly. Funny that water that looked almost black from the air could be so clear when you were in it.

They started swimming away from the plane, J. B., Mr. Sperber, and Matthew all taking turns helping the injured pilot. Matthew soon realized as he kicked along that his tennis shoes were going to give him trouble, so he scraped them off one by one and let them sink.

They swam about twenty feet before stopping to look back. The plane had slipped below the water, but they could still see it hovering just beneath the surface. Like Matthew's bass, it seemed to hesitate for a moment and then suddenly tilt downward.

Matthew watched bleakly as the plane slid down and away from them through the crystal-clear water, growing smaller and smaller. He kept staring until it had spiraled all the way out of sight into the black depths below. For some reason, having the plane floating there with them had been comforting. Now they were alone in the sea.

When he finally looked up, the others' faces told him that they felt the loss, too. After a moment Mr. Langford cleared his throat.

"Gentlemen," he said weakly. "I've been an ordained minister for the last twenty-five years. Why don't we pray together?"

Matthew closed his eyes as the frail minister-pilot offered a simple prayer for their rescue. Maybe it would help; maybe it wouldn't. But it sure couldn't hurt at this point.

Soon his father took charge. "Let's hook our life jackets together," he suggested. "There's a really strong current out here, and we don't want to get separated." Matthew weaved a cord from Mr. Sperber's jacket through his own waist cord, then together they splashed over to J. B. to tie his life jacket to theirs. Now none of them could drift off without the others.

J. B. was supporting the injured pilot in his bear-like arms. "Mike," he said, "he's still bleeding pretty bad from that bang he got on his head. He's going to need some help to stay afloat."

Matthew looked over, noticing that Mr. Langford's hair was thickly matted with blood and that his shirt collar was also bloodstained.

Mr. Sperber raised an eyebrow. "What about the graycoats?" He asked in a low tone.

Matthew frowned, puzzled. What was he talking about? Then suddenly he understood. *Blood in the water.*

His father was saying "graycoats" instead of sharks to keep from scaring the injured pilot. He shot a sudden, uneasy glance down into the water where his bare legs and feet dangled. Sharks were supposed to be able to sense blood from miles away. He pictured the dark waters thousands of feet below, where his tennis shoes had dropped just minutes before. What if they'd drawn the attention of—?

Stop it! he ordered himself angrily, forcing his eyes away from the water. If a shark was going to attack them, he'd rather not see it coming.

J. B. had understood Mr. Sperber's words. "Uh, Mike, I think we'd best not talk about that," he said. "What can we do about Jerry?"

Mr. Sperber thought for just a moment. "Okay, Jerry," he finally said. "Take off your pants."

Matthew stared and asked, "Why do you want him to do *that*?"

"It's a navy trick. You can make a great float out of a pair of pants if you know how."

"Oh." Matthew looked away, embarrassed, as Mr. Langford struggled out of his pants and held them up. They were some kind of old-guy pants, probably twenty years old.

Mr. Sperber looked at them doubtfully. "I don't know if it'll work with double-knit pants, but we can give it a try."

He knotted the bottom of each leg, then held them open at the waistband. "Scooping" the pants quickly overhead to fill them with air, he plunged them upside-down into the water and held them there, using the water to seal off the open waistband. The legs stuck up slightly puffed.

"Now, splash some water up inside the legs," he told Matthew.

Matthew wondered how on earth that was going to help. But as he plunged his cupped hands into the water again and again, scooping handfuls of water up into the pants, small air bubbles were also trapped. The legs slowly grew rounder, sticking up like a person doing a headstand.

"There," Mr. Sperber finally said. "I think that's as good as it's going to get. Now we'll just have to see how bad they leak." He looked at Mr. Langford. "You'll need to climb on and straddle the pants legs, kind of like riding a horse. Your weight will hold the top down so the air won't escape. If they don't leak, they'll hold you up almost forever."

He added to Matthew, "That's why the navy makes sailors wear bell-bottom jeans. In an emergency your pants or even your cap can make a great float."

"I never knew that," Matthew said. "That's neat."

Mr. Langford crawled onto the inflated pants, but they went flat almost immediately.

"Well, so much for that," Mr. Sperber said. "Maybe we can make a sling out of the pants instead."

After trying several different arrangements, they settled on one where Matthew and J. B. tied a pants leg to each of their life jackets to make a kind of hammock. The pilot sat on that and rested his head on Mr. Sperber's jacket. It seemed to keep everybody's faces, at least, above the water.

The sun was edging lower in the sky, sending brilliant orange and red reflections across the water.

Matthew shifted uncomfortably. His plastic life jacket was cutting into his neck, and his eyes were stinging from the salt water. He glanced at his dive watch wondering how long they'd been in the water. He was surprised to see that it was barely seven o'clock.

"Dad, why isn't anybody here yet?" he asked.

"I'm sure they're on their way. We got out at least one distress call that somebody should've heard. The Coast Guard's probably working on it."

"I hope they find us soon. I'm thirsty."

"Think about something else."

Matthew smiled wryly. *Yeah,* he thought, *like sharks. Or maybe a nice big hurricane. That would get my mind off being thirsty pretty fast.*

They drifted for a while in silence, pushed along by the Gulf Stream current. At first Matthew didn't notice the faint sound, a kind of rhythmic *thup-thup-thup* in the distance. Finally he said, "What's that sound?"

Mr. Sperber listened. "I don't hear anything." J. B. and the pilot also shook their heads.

"Can't you hear it? It's getting louder." Matthew listened again, then peered up into the sky. "Look!" he said excitedly, pointing to a dark speck south of them. "A helicopter! See it? It's coming right at us!"

Now all of them could hear it. They stared up, straining their eyes. As it drew closer, they were able to pick out the red and white markings on its side. Mr. Sperber let out a whoop.

"It's the Coast Guard!" he yelled. "We're out of here!"

Flying at low speed, the helicopter made a beeline for them. They all yelled and waved, certain that they'd been spotted— and watched in stunned disbelief as it passed right over them and kept going. Their happy shouts died. Somehow the searchers had missed them.

"Why didn't they see us?" Matthew demanded in frustration. "They were right on top of us!"

"From the air, we're just little specks," Mr. Sperber said slowly. "Without a way to signal . . ."

Matthew leaned back against his life jacket, no longer caring that water was getting in his ears. If the searchers hadn't seen them when it was light outside, they sure weren't going to see them at night. He watched in silence as the sun went down.

///

Within an hour after learning of the plane crash Mrs. Sperber had started calling everybody she knew who owned their own planes or boats. Her husband and son were stranded somewhere out in the Atlantic. They needed to be found!

Soon her living room was crowded with friends and family who all joined the effort. Dozens of private boats headed out to sea, and so many small-plane pilots showed up at the airport wanting to join the search that the Coast Guard had to start turning them away.

Through it all, Adam remained unusually quiet. He couldn't stop thinking about his dad and Matthew. What if they were dead? Huddled in his father's favorite recliner, he blinked back the tears that were stinging his eyes. He kept remembering all the times he'd blown up at Matthew or shrugged off chances to go fishing with his dad. He wished now he could take them all back.

Don't be dead, he pleaded silently. *I love you guys.*

Night Falls on the Atlantic

The time passed slowly for the foursome in the water. They watched in frustration as planes and helicopters crisscrossed the skies to the south and east of them. Bright searchlights darted back and forth across the dark water and search boats bobbed along the surface. But none of them even came close.

Matthew finally grew sleepy. He would have dozed off, but his dad kept reminding him not to.

"Your eyes and ears are a lot sharper than ours," he said. "You heard that helicopter coming a long time before any of the rest of us did. We need you to stay alert and tell us if you see or hear anything."

Matthew was surprised but pleased. "Okay, Dad," he said. "I'll do it." After that he made sure to keep his ears clear of water.

As the night wore on, the water grew cool, then cold. Matthew shivered, fighting to keep his eyes open. The sky overhead was crowded with stars, the water solid black. It would probably be beautiful if they'd been looking at it from the deck of a nice, comfortable boat.

It took an effort to keep his mind off thoughts of the huge predators that moved through those dark waters. Every time he started thinking about them he could almost feel the presence of something large rushing toward him, unseen, ready to tug him under. It sent shudders up his spine. To distract himself he let his mind drift back over the events of the past five days.

Staying at Rosie's—now that had been great. He couldn't wait to show his mom and Adam all the pictures they'd taken—he stopped there abruptly. His dad's camera had been in the plane. That, and everything else they'd brought, was now at the bottom of the ocean.

The crash. It was like every detail was burned into his brain. He remembered the sharp bang as the first engine quit and the sudden silence after the second engine died. He remembered the sick feeling in his stomach as they plunged downward and the sight of the waves rushing up to meet them.

He also remembered, with some surprise, the moment just before the crash when he'd screamed, "Dad, I love you!" That was really strange. If anybody had asked him before if he loved his father he probably would've said, "I guess so" just to be polite; secretly, though, he would've been doubtful. He and his dad did things together, but that was it. They never really talked about love and stuff like that.

Then he recalled the expression on his father's face when he'd told him not to wait for him or anyone, to get out of the plane as soon as it stopped. In that moment, he'd seen clearly how his dad felt about him—and even more startling, how he really felt about his dad.

He loved him. Strange.

And now his dad and the others were counting on him to be their "eyes and ears." Matthew determined not to let them down.

Although he kept a careful watch, however, none of the search planes came anywhere near them throughout the long night. Toward dawn, as the sky gradually lightened to grey, then turned rosy pink, the searchers were still far off to the south.

At first Matthew was relieved to have the sun up again; the ocean seemed much less threatening in daylight, and he was freezing. But as the morning wore on, the sun turned sweltering. All of their faces and lips began to redden and blister.

It was worst for Mr. Langford, who had pale skin and no stubble on his chin. Within hours his face was burned almost purple. He rarely spoke. His head injury had left him weak and confused.

J. B. finally shook his head. "This is miserable." His ruddy cheeks were flushed and deeply burned. Like the others, his arms and hands were puffy and wrinkled from being underwater.

Mike Sperber nodded. "I think I'm going to rip the pocket off my T-shirt to put on my forehead."

"Good idea. Me, too." Soon all four of them were ripping off their pockets and wetting them down to plaster across their heads and faces. It helped a little.

Matthew sighed, licking his dry lips. His mouth tasted dry and salty, and he was both hungry and thirsty. He had raw spots on the sides of his neck where his life jacket had rubbed repeatedly against his bare skin. He kept trying to scoot his T-shirt up to cover his neck, but it wouldn't stay. He pressed his burned lips together to keep them out of the sun.

Lifting a water-puckered hand to shield his eyes, he scanned the blue sky for the hundredth time. All the search planes and boats were still staying off to the south and east. Why didn't they move this way?

It was close to noon when Matthew finally heard something. "Dad! A plane's coming!" he called. They soon spotted it—a Coast Guard aircraft. As the plane got closer, Mr. Sperber identified it as a C-130. They all began to splash and wave. It was heading straight for them.

About a mile away, the plane dropped down abruptly to fly closer to the water. Was it signalling that it had seen them? They waved harder, almost afraid to hope after the disappointment the night before. Was this it?

Suddenly, the plane banked off to the west. Mr. Sperber froze, and then slowly lowered his arms. "It didn't see us," he said flatly. "It's just flying a grid pattern."

Matthew's heart sank. As he looked around at the others, though, he suddenly felt even sorrier for them than he did for himself. He was young and strong, at least. His dad was in pretty good shape, but he was still old. J. B. was overweight and the pilot was hurt. This had to be much harder on them.

"At least they're starting to come this way now," he said. It was the only encouraging thing he could think of to say. "The next one will probably be it."

But after a noisy turboprop lumbered past directly overhead without seeing them it was hard to keep pretending. Matthew leaned back for a moment to rest his eyes. Eventually, somebody would stumble across them. They *had* to!

"Look!" Mr. Sperber shouted in excitement. "A boat!"

Matthew sat up and stared out across the flat sea. Sure enough, a huge sportfishing boat was cruising toward them. Even from that distance he could pick out several people up on the tuna tower. A faint sound of music carried across the water.

"Hey!" Matthew screamed, cupping his hands around his mouth. "Help!"

The others all joined in, screaming and waving. Soon the boat was close enough to see the people on the tower. A man and woman were relaxing in lounge chairs, drinks in hand, listening to a radio. They had the music cranked all the way up.

"Over here!" J. B. bellowed. "*Over here!*"

Matthew put his fingers in his mouth and let loose an ear-splitting whistle. *If they didn't hear that,* he thought, *they're deaf!* But the boat, just one hundred yards away, showed no signs of slowing down.

The four in the water were almost hysterical. "*Help!*" they screamed. "You've got to stop! Help us!"

The sunbathers never even looked up. The boat cruised away and the music slowly faded.

Matthew felt stunned. He had been so sure that they'd be rescued this time. He swallowed hard, wanting to cry. It was too much.

His dad noticed his sudden silence. "Hey," he said heavily, "don't worry about it. You're a tough kid. We're going to make it through okay."

J. B. reached over to pat his shoulder. "Yeah. You're really something, Matthew. Not a whimper out of you this whole time. That's more than a lot of grown men could've done."

Matthew was embarrassed. "Whimpering wouldn't do any good."

J. B. smiled, his swollen lips cracking. "That's true, but it doesn't stop a lot of people. Right, Mike?"

"Yep. But that's one thing about Matthew: he's always been able to pull his own weight. I've always been able to count on him just like one of the guys."

His dad looked at him and nodded. Matthew smiled back, not knowing what to say.

The afternoon wore on, growing more sweltering with each hour. Matthew finally decided to take off his thick cotton underwear and drape them over his head and face. He'd considered using his shorts but decided he didn't like the idea of floating in his underwear. And what would happen when they were rescued? He'd rather have pants on, thank you.

Wriggling out of his shorts, he quickly pulled off his underwear, then replaced his shorts. When he put the dripping underwear on his head, he sighed with relief. It might look stupid, but he could always sink his underwear when the rescuers finally came. Right now it felt great, his Fruit-of-the-Loom™ hat.

Hours passed without any boat or plane sightings. The sun beat down on them unmercifully. By mid-afternoon the four in the water were miserable with heat and thirst.

"I'll tell you what," J. B. said with a sigh. "I'd gladly pay five hundred dollars cash for a gallon of water."

Mike nodded. "I'd probably even go *six* hundred," he said, making a weak joke. "And it'd be worth every penny."

"Seven hundred," J. B. said quickly, making it into an auction. He patted his back pocket. "Got it right here in my wallet."

"Eight hundred," Mike countered. "I've got five hundred dollars on me, but I've got more at home."

Matthew smiled at Mr. Langford. *Too bad,* he thought, *that I didn't bring a gallon of water. Of course, if I had, I wouldn't part with it, not for a million dollars.*

"Forget those little bids," J. B. said haughtily. "And forget that stuff about getting more money from home, Mike. I'll go a full thousand dollars. Either put up or shut up."

Mr. Sperber shrugged. "Okay, okay. You win."

Suddenly Matthew yelped, and they both turned to stare at him. Something had brushed against the side of his leg! Startled, he looked down to see a school of barjacks, small silvery bait fish, darting all around his legs.

"Hey!" he said. "What'll you guys give me if I catch a fish?" He'd never eaten raw fish, but he was hungry enough now to try it.

Mr. Sperber smiled. "I guess that'd be worth about fifty bucks."

Matthew nodded. Slowly, carefully, he moved his hands over the water. One barjack was swimming close to the surface. If he could just nab it. . .

Suddenly he plunged both hands into the water and grabbed at the small fish. It easily darted away, and the rest of the school also scattered and fled.

"Oh, well," Matthew said. "They probably would've tasted bad anyway."

They drifted in silence after that, too tired and miserable even to talk. No other planes or boats came their way. As the sun once again dipped low on the horizon, they realized with sinking hearts that they were going to face another night in the dark water.

"How long do you think they'll keep looking for us?" Matthew asked. The lights from the search planes and boats in the distance seemed to be thinning out. What if they just called off the search, figuring they were all dead?

"They'll keep looking till they find us," Mr. Sperber assured him.

Matthew felt relieved for a moment—but he wondered if his father was lying to make him feel better. The Coast Guard *did* sometimes call off searches without finding people; he had seen things like that in the paper. He blinked his sun-swollen eyes and swallowed painfully, longing for even a tiny sip of fresh water.

As midnight approached the ocean once again grew chilly. Matthew started shivering uncontrollably. The night before he had still had a lot of energy to fight the cold; now, weak and dehydrated, he couldn't even stop his teeth from chattering. The thought of the hours ahead made him feel even weaker. How could he stand it? Why didn't the rescuers come and find them? He could hardly keep his eyes open.

He was drifting along, only half-awake, when something hit his left arm like a hot razor blade. He screamed and flailed in the water.

"What's wrong?" His dad shouted. "Matthew, what's wrong?"

"Something's on my arm!" he shrieked.

Clawing at his skin in a panic, Matthew felt something slick and stringy wrapped tightly around his arm—tentacles! He shoved them away in a panic, but not before another sharp jolt of pain hit him. He screamed again.

His dad and the others fought to pull Matthew away from his unseen attacker. As Mike blindly pawed at the water, a tentacle slid across his face, delivering a burning sting to his cheek. The searing pain revealed what they were facing: a Portuguese man-of-war!

The man-of-war was a large jellyfish-like creature that lived in the warm waters off the Florida coast. Resembling a purplish balloon, it floated along on the surface trailing poisonous tentacles, some as long as thirty feet. It killed its prey—fish, usually—by stinging and paralyzing them.

Matthew was sobbing with fear and pain, twisting and splashing to escape the stinging tentacles. Mr. Sperber yelled, "It's a man-of-war! We need to swim out of its reach!"

Working together, he and the other two men managed to drag Matthew out of the creature's clutches. But the wounds on the teenager's arm, raw welts injected with poison, continued to burn like wasp stings. Matthew couldn't stop crying.

"Dad," he sobbed hysterically, "I'm cold and I'm tired and I'm thirsty. I want to go home. I don't want to die out here!"

Mr. Sperber pulled him close. "None of us wants to die, and none of us are going to. *They're going to find us.* You hear me? They're going to find us!"

Matthew looked up, barely able to see through his tears. In the moonlight, his father's sun-blistered face was tinged with blue.

"Matthew, I—" Mr. Sperber's voice faltered. "I never really tell you that I love you, but I hope you know that I do. You're something really special to me." He hesitated, then finished awkwardly, "I—well, I just wanted to tell you that."

His words helped Matthew calm down. He finally drew a shaky breath. "I know," he said, still clutching his wounded arm. He leaned back against his father's arm, comforted to know that no matter what happened, they'd be together.

Waiting for Rescue

The Sperbers' living room was still crowded at one o'clock in the morning. Friends, relatives, and search organizers had been camping out there since Sunday night, sure that at any moment they would hear that the missing crash victims had been found. Mrs. Sperber hadn't been able to eat or sleep although it had already been thirty-three hours since her husband and son disappeared.

The TV news reports were growing increasingly gloomy. The area where the plane was thought to have gone down had been searched again and again with no sign of survivors. A life jacket had been found floating several miles away, but it had turned out to be from a boat. It seemed more and more likely that the plane and all its occupants had disappeared beneath the waves. There was talk of calling off the search the following day.

Adam wandered around the house trying to stay out of everybody's way. He didn't know what to say to all the adults who kept asking, "Are you all right?" or trying to make him eat. He usually mumbled, "I'm okay," but he didn't mean it. How could he be all right?

His mother wasn't all right, either. She paced around all the time, trying her best not to cry—probably for his sake. He finally went to her and gave her a solemn hug.

"Mom, you can cry on my shoulder if you need to," he said quietly. "It's okay."

She hugged him back so hard that it almost hurt. "Oh, Adam, I don't know what I'd do without you right now. This is all such a nightmare."

Several times Adam wandered into Matthew's room and sat on his bed. His brother's guitar was still propped in the corner next to his stack of CD's. Would he ever be back to play it again? Walking over to Matthew's dresser, he picked up the small framed picture of his dad and Matthew holding a big jack they'd caught. He stared at it for a long moment, studying their happy faces, before abruptly turning the picture facedown. He felt like his throat was going to swell closed if he cried any more.

"Please, God," he whispered. "Please bring them back home."

/ / /

Miles away, the foursome in the water were barely hanging on. Despite Matthew's efforts to stay awake and alert, he kept dozing off. He was delirious with thirst, tormented by the stabbing pain in his arm. He kept jerking back awake, terrified that he might have missed a passing plane or boat.

In his first waking moments, he was sure that he saw a plane once, and another time a brightly lit ocean liner. As soon as he blinked his eyes, though, they disappeared. He felt sick to his stomach and dizzy. His eyes kept turning helplessly to the distant search planes criss crossing the sky, looking in all the wrong places. Why didn't they come?

It was almost two o'clock Tuesday morning when he awoke to see a boat just one hundred feet away. As he stared, a dusky-skinned man on the deck glanced up, and then started waving excitedly. He'd seen them!

"Dad!" he gasped. "Dad! He sees us!"

"Who sees us?" Mr. Sperber asked dully.

"That guy in the boat! Look!"

Mr. Sperber twisted all around in the water. "Matthew, there's nobody here. You must be dreaming."

"I'm not dreaming," Matthew protested. "Can't you see him? He's right over—"

But even as he pointed, he saw the dark, empty water. His father was right. Nothing was there. He settled back with a weary sigh.

Over the next few hours, they all drifted in and out of a miserable half-dozing state, too cold to sleep and too exhausted to stay awake. None of them felt much like talking. Mr. Langford, the weakest of the four, groaned and mumbled. He wasn't going to last much longer.

During one of his more alert moments, Matthew thought about his mother and Adam. *Mom's probably calling everybody we know to make them come out and look for us,* he decided. The thought was comforting. *Even if the Coast Guard gave up, Mom wouldn't.*

And Adam . . . he was probably really upset. Still, Matthew was glad his little brother was with his mom. Adam was a lot like her; he felt a lot more than he showed. He always seemed to know what to say when she was down.

Picturing home sent a sudden wave of homesickness washing over Matthew. He couldn't think about it right now; it hurt too bad. He glanced around, seeing how peaceful everything looked in the cool moonlight. The water stretched out dark and smooth as far as he could see with barely a ripple to disturb it. Again he stifled the images of dark horrors lurking just beneath the peaceful surface. Whatever was going to happen was going to happen. Worrying about it would only make it worse.

Next to him, Mr. Sperber was gently swishing his hands back and forth, watching as the phosporous in the water made his wedding ring and heavy gold bracelet glow a bright green. If a plane came over at night, would they be able to see that? Probably not, he thought. But suddenly he realized how it must look from the depths below. What if it attracted predators? He decided to slip off his jewelry and hide it in his pocket.

He was clutching his ring and bracelet in his hand when an idea struck him.

"Hey!" he said, startling Matthew and the others out of their reverie. "I wonder if we take all our jewelry and put it with the metal carbon dioxide cartridges from our lifejackets, could that be picked up by radar? I could wave it all around next time a plane flies over. Maybe if they see something moving on the radar they'll come back for another look."

"It might work," J. B. said. "And you know, I was just thinking about something else. It wouldn't work at night, but once the sun comes up we might be able to use our credit cards to flash a signal. You know, a lot of cards have those shiny holograms on them now. I know my Visa™ card does."

"My Visa has a hologram, too," Mike replied. "That's a great idea!"

Matthew felt his hopes rising. He glanced at his watch. It was a few minutes after four. The sun would be rising in another couple hours.

But dawn, when it finally came, was disappointing. Instead of rising bright and hot, the sun peeped out weakly from behind dark, heavy-looking clouds. Soon the wind picked up, and the air grew even cooler. As the sky darkened, the flat ocean surface broke into ripples, then waves. Whitecaps began to form all around them, leaving them bobbing around in increasingly rough seas.

When thunder rumbled in the distance, J. B. pressed his lips together. "Just what we need," he said grimly.

Matthew looked up at the approaching storm clouds and then reached over to get a better grip on the injured pilot. If the man was tossed away from them in the stormy waves, he'd never make it without a life jacket.

Mr. Langford roused and turned his blistered, swollen face to gaze at them through dull eyes. "Maybe we ought to have a little group prayer," he said hoarsely. As the storm swept upon them they once again prayed together for rescue.

/ / /

Mrs. Sperber woke up early Tuesday morning after tossing and turning for a few hours. The sky outside was grey and depressing. She stared out the window, chewing her lip. Where were Matthew and Mike right now? Were they somewhere out in the vast Atlantic, looking up at that same sky? Or were they dead, trapped in plane wreckage along the dark sea bottom?

Oh, God, please. . . . She had prayed so many times now that she didn't have any words left. Tears stung her eyes. There must be something she could do to help them. There *must* be!

Suddenly, she felt a restless urging to get out of the house. Adam had gone over to his grandparents' house around the corner. She dressed quickly and called a neighbor, knowing she was too distracted to drive. When the neighbor arrived, Mrs. Sperber blurted out, "I want to go to a church."

A few minutes later they pulled into the parking lot of her friend's church, Trinity Assembly. Mrs. Sperber had never been much of a churchgoer, but now, somehow, it's what she wanted to do.

She quickly found the pastor, a big man with brown hair and glasses and a kind voice. He nodded sympathetically when she told him who she was; he told her that he had heard about the missing plane on the news.

"Would you like me to pray with you?" the pastor asked.

Mrs. Sperber nodded tearfully. "I've been praying at home, but I just feel like it isn't good enough."

The minister took her hand and bowed his head.

"Lord, I know that you see even the tiniest sparrow that falls from the sky," he prayed, "and that nothing happens without your knowledge. Right now, I just ask that your eye will be on Mrs. Sperber's loved ones, wherever they are. . . ."

The Third Day

The storm beat upon the four in the water with great fury. As heavy raindrops pelted them and cold waves tossed them up and down, Matthew clung tightly to the others. Desperate for a drink, he tried to catch some of the rain in his mouth, but choked when the salty waves slapped him in the face. Throughout the storm he never relaxed his grip on Mr. Langford even though the effort made his wounded arm ache unbearably.

Finally, the storm swept past them and headed away. The rain clouds slowly cleared and the seas once again became calm. When the sun appeared, they all lifted their faces gratefully to its light and warmth. Off in the distance they could see several search helicopters returning. It was a relief to know people were still looking for them, even if they were searching in the wrong place.

/ / /

"Adam, can I talk to you for a minute?"

Adam nodded and followed his Grandpa Sperber back to his room. The old man's face was lined with grief and his hands were shaking. When he sat down on the edge of the bed, Adam sat beside him. "I know this is going to be hard," his grandfather said, "but I think it's time that we talked about some things." He stopped, then plunged on. "It looks like you're the man of the house now, with your dad and brother gone, and—"

"Grandpa, they're not gone," Adam said quickly. "They'll be okay. Don't worry about it."

"Adam." Grandpa Sperber shook his head. "You need to face the facts, son. We all do. It's about time we all decide on some funeral arrangements."

"No!" Adam jumped up, agitated. "We can't give up on them. You know Dad. He'd *never* give up. They're going to be okay."

/ / /

Matthew's head jerked up. He sat up in the water. "I hear a plane," he announced. "It's coming this way!"

In the heat of the morning sun Matthew had once again donned his underwear hat. Mr. Sperber scanned the sky anxiously.

"Are you sure?" he asked. "I don't see anything."

"It sounds like a jet." An instant later Matthew pointed triumphantly. "Look, there it is!" Sure enough, a silver jet was roaring toward them from the south, flying a low grid pattern.

They all tensed. This might be their last chance to be spotted. As planned, Mr. Sperber quickly gathered his jewelry and everybody's carbon dioxide cartridges and held them bunched in one hand. In his other hand he held his Visa card, ready to flash. J. B. pulled out his own charge card.

Matthew looked around in frustration. What could *he* do to signal? He didn't have a charge card or anything shiny to flash and he wasn't wearing any jewelry. Then he had an idea.

"Dad, why don't we untie our lifejackets and spread out a little? Maybe they'll see us better that way."

"No!" Mr. Sperber exclaimed sharply. "We have to stay together."

The jet was almost upon them. Mr. Sperber held the metal objects up with one hand and moved them around in a box-like pattern, using his other hand to tilt his Visa card back and forth in the sunlight. J. B. also flashed his Visa card and yelled. Mr. Langford used both hands to wave.

Matthew hesitated before quickly slipping out of his life jacket. Hanging onto the cords, he let his legs drift out away from the others, then started kicking and splashing as hard as he could. *Maybe,* he thought, *the white foam will catch the pilot's eye.*

Seconds later the jet screamed past directly above them, drowning out their desperate cries. Without any sign of having spotted them, it disappeared off toward the north.

They stared, silently begging it to return. Two minutes, then three minutes, passed. Nothing. J. B. finally said, "If they don't find us now, they never will."

But Matthew wasn't listening. He was straining his ears for something else. "It's coming back!" he yelled. "The jet's coming back!"

This time, nobody asked him if he was sure. A moment later they all heard it—the returning scream of the search jet. When they spotted it they saw that it was flying back over the exact same grid line.

"Everybody splash!" Matthew shouted. Once again he started thrashing the water into a white foam. This time the others splashed along waving their arms, jewelry, and credit cards.

When the jet got closer, Mr. Sperber said triumphantly, "They've turned their landing lights on! They see us!"

Once again, however, the jet roared over above their heads and disappeared again, back toward the south. What was going on?

Matthew was trembling, straining to listen. Mr. Sperber and the others held their breaths and stared at him hopefully. Was it coming back?

Then Matthew's eyes widened and his sunburned face broke into a huge grin. "It's coming back!" he screamed. "All *right!* It's coming back!"

This time, when the jet reappeared it was flying so slow that it seemed to be barely hanging in the air. It followed the same grid line back toward them; but as it flew directly overhead they saw the hatch open. A metal cannister fell down toward the water.

"A smoke cannister!" Mr. Sperber yelled. "They're dropping a marker!"

Matthew laughed with excitement as he watched the cannister hit the waves, then detonate, sending a long streamer of smoke up into the sky. The jet roared away again, this time at full speed.

Less than five minutes later Matthew heard the *thup-thup-thup* of a helicopter racing toward them.

/ / /

Adam was still talking to his grandfather when the phone rang out in the living room. His aunt answered it and started screaming for Adam. He jumped up and ran out into the hall.

His aunt was grinning from ear to ear. "Adam!" she shouted, sweeping him up in a big hug. "Your dad and Matthew have been found. They're both okay!"

"All *right!*" Adam yelled, jumping up into the air. "All right! All right!"

Suddenly to his surprise, he burst into tears. He was still sobbing several minutes later when his mom arrived to take him to St. Mary's Hospital, where the four crash survivors were being taken.

/ / /

Matthew almost felt like he was walking through a dream as he, his dad, J. B. Stephens, and Mr. Langford all climbed into the medical van to be taken to St. Mary's. The flight crew had given each of them something to drink, which had helped a lot. After floating for days in the ocean, it seemed strange to do normal things like sit in a van. The thought of a hot shower and dry clothes were almost overwhelming. Not to mention hot food!

They had learned that when the jet crew first spotted them in the water, they had thought it was probably a sea turtle splashing along. Matthew's idea to kick up a lot of foam had worked to catch their eye and bring them back for a second look.

When the medical van pulled into St. Mary's, a small mob was waiting to greet them. Matthew stepped out first—and almost staggered as his mother and Adam flung themselves at him with a joyful cry. Mr. Sperber stepped out and joined them as they clung there together laughing and crying and hugging. Nearby, J. B. and Mr. Langford were being greeted by their own friends and families.

Matthew reached out to put one sun-blistered arm around his mother and the other around Adam. Looking from his father's burned, stubbly face to the tearful faces of his mother and little brother, he suddenly felt weak and near tears himself.

It is good, he thought, *to have a family. And no matter what else happened, that was one thing he wasn't likely to ever forget.*

Blinded at Big Hole

The Colleen Cooke Story

A paper-ball whizzed past Mrs. Stevenson's desk at Victor Elementary School, accompanied by a squeal of childish laughter. The teacher smiled calmly, scanning the room of wiggling, jubilant fourth-graders. It was Friday, May 29, 1987, the last day of school. Who could expect the kids to sit and wait patiently for the final bell? "Sara!" shrieked Colleen Cooke, as she was grappling with a giggling red-haired boy who was

61

trying to snatch her lunchbox. "Come and help me!" Sara ran over to help her tug it out of the boy's grasp.

Colleen, nine, was the daughter of the school's popular third-grade teacher, Jannifer Cooke. The young students had watched with great curiosity over the last nine months as Mrs. Cooke slowly "got fat"—particularly around her stomach. Colleen had explained without enthusiasm that her mother was going to have a baby.

"I don't know why she wants one," she'd told Sara in disgust. "It's just going to be a lot of bother. Crying, diapers, all that stuff."

"But won't it be neat to have a baby brother or sister?" Sara asked.

"No," Colleen said shortly. "I've got Casey, my dad's little brother—that's all I need. I don't like babies."

Now, as the bell pealed, there was a united cheer. Colleen yelled, "Bye, Mrs. Stevenson!" and charged for the door with the others. After telling a few other friends good-bye she walked over to her mom's classroom.

Mrs. Cooke was cleaning out her desk. "Hi, honey," she said tiredly. "How'd your classroom party go?"

"Fine! We had cupcakes and stuff." Colleen glanced around. "You want me to put the chairs up on the desks for you?"

"I'd appreciate it. I tell you what, if I don't have this baby soon I think I'm going to pop. I never expected a second baby to be late like this."

Colleen didn't answer. This baby wasn't even born yet and it was already a troublemaker. If her mom and dad had wanted something else bawling around the house they should've just bought another calf.

But a few minutes later, pulling into the driveway at home, Colleen felt more cheerful. Summertime was here at last!

"You'd better go right now and feed Blackie," Mrs. Cooke reminded her as they got out of the car. "Your father's going to have a fit if you forget again."

Blackie was a young steer Mr. Cooke had bought for Colleen to raise and sell that fall. Blackie had weighed about five hundred pounds when they'd gotten him the month before, but by that August he'd be up over nine hundred pounds. Since he would sell for one dollar per pound, Colleen would be left with about a four-hundred-dollar profit after subtracting costs.

Her father said she could spend the money however she wanted—but only if she took care of Blackie without being reminded. So far, that hadn't worked out too well.

"I just wish Blackie wasn't so mean," Colleen sighed. "He kind of scares me."

"It'll be easier once you learn to handle him. Then he'll come when you call him and follow you around like a little pet." She smiled. "Well, maybe a *big* pet. Anyway, you have to watch that you don't get too attached to him since he'll be sold for beef."

"I'll *never* get attached to that dumb old steer! I'd sell him right now if I could."

"Well, you can't. Go feed him."

Colleen walked over to the small yard where Blackie was kept, forked some fresh hay into his trough, and poured some grain from a bucket into a smaller trough. As usual, Blackie snorted and retreated across the yard to glare at her, his dark eyes hostile. After checking his water, she stuck her tongue out at him and headed for the kennel to let the dogs out.

When she swung open the gate, Sam, their aging golden retriever, bounded out happily to greet her. Andy, Mr. Cooke's German shepherd, was a little less excited. Colleen played with them both for a few minutes and then went inside.

The Cooke's house, situated on a quiet country road with six other homes, was made of logs. But it wasn't anything like the log cabins most people expected. It had three stories, including the basement, and a rock fireplace that extended from the basement all the way up to the second story. Colleen's bedroom and bathroom were on the top floor next to the TV room. She loved having her own area like that, practically all to herself.

Stomping up the steps, she tossed her school stuff onto her bed. The bed and headboard had been her mother's graduation present many years before; many of the Barbies™ stacked in her dollhouse had also been her mother's. She straightened several of them, wondering resentfully if her mom would take them back to give the new baby if it turned out to be a girl.

She'd better not, she thought. *If she tries to take any of them I'll just go feed them to Blackie. The new kid can have whatever's left.*

It was a little after six o'clock when Mr. Cooke arrived home from work. A strong, wiry man with a drooping mustache, Kim Cooke was the sheriff of all Teton County, Idaho. He was also a skilled rodeo contestant. He had taught Colleen how to ride and show horses and even a little about roping. He could skillfully toss a noose over a running calf; now Colleen could rope fence posts out in the yard. Mr. Cooke liked to tease that someday, if she was lucky, she might be able to rope large rocks—as long as they held still.

Colleen was helping her mom set the table when her father strode in. He grinned at her and then turned to his wife.

"Haven't you had that baby *yet?*" he teased. He kissed her warmly before reaching over to tousle Colleen's hair. "Hey, how's it feel to be out of school? I guess I'm gonna have to get used to all your scummy little friends hanging around here all the time again."

Colleen smiled impishly. "Yep. I told them all you said they could come over whenever they wanted." She dodged as he aimed a playful swat at her behind.

When dinner was ready they each served their plates and disappeared to their favorite spots. Mr. Cooke and Colleen went upstairs to the TV room while Mrs. Cooke stayed downstairs to eat at the table. With her pregnant tummy, it was hard to balance a plate on her lap—or even, for that matter, to get up the stairs. This baby was certainly in no hurry to be born!

Late that night, Colleen laid awake thinking excitedly about what she'd do the next day. Casey, her father's fourteen-year-old brother, would be coming over while his parents—her grandparents—went to a big cattle sale in a neighboring town. Casey had always been more like an older brother than an uncle to her. She was glad her grandparents' ranch was close enough so she and Casey could play together.

We can probably ride the four-wheeler around, she mused dreamily. *That'll be fun.* With those happy thoughts she drifted off to sleep.

The next morning dawned clear and beautiful. Colleen jumped up and ran downstairs. She was hurrying through breakfast, anxious to get started on the day, when her father walked in.

"It's a perfect day outside, clear and cool," he said, zipping up his yellow sweatshirt. "What do you say we go for a horse ride?"

Colleen's heart sank. She usually liked riding with her dad, but today she just wasn't in the mood. She'd been looking forward to playing with Casey.

When she looked up at her father's face, though, she couldn't bring herself to tell him that. "Uh, okay," she said. "I'll be there in a minute."

The phone rang and Mr. Cooke answered it. After he hung up, he turned to Colleen apologetically.

"There's been an accident with a fatality. I've got to go. We'll have to wait on that ride until I get back."

Colleen tried to conceal her relief. "That's okay. I've got other stuff to do around here anyway."

Her father grinned. "You're a good kid. I'll try to hurry."

Don't, Colleen thought. *Take a-l-l the time you want.* The minute he left she turned to her mother. "I don't want to go riding with Dad today," she complained. "I was looking forward to playing with Casey."

"You need to go, honey. Your dad doesn't get that much time with you and he really enjoys it. Besides, you'll hurt his feelings if you tell him that."

"I know. That's why I didn't say anything. But I wish he'd find something else to do so I could stay here."

Casey arrived a few minutes later, roaring up on his small motorcycle. Andy and Sam raced around the yard, barking, as Colleen ran out to greet him. Soon Colleen and Casey were looking at the four-wheeler, an off-road vehicle like a small jeep. They were just getting ready to go out in it when Mr. Cooke's car pulled back into the driveway.

"Hi, Casey," he said cheerfully. "Come on, Colleen. Let's go catch the horses and get out of here before I get another call."

Colleen sighed. She'd be stuck with dumb old Cammie, her grandfather's horse. Her own beautiful horse, Dollar, had died several months before of a heart attack. Cammie was ugly and slow as a mule. Colleen followed her dad with dragging steps.

They caught the horses and were getting ready to saddle them when her mother called from the front door: "Kim, it's the telephone! It's your office."

Mr. Cooke made an exasperated sound and stomped into the house. A moment later, when he came back out, he had his car keys in hand.

"Can you believe this?" he said. "I've got to go again. Somebody hit a deer and dented their car." He shook his head. "Go ahead and leave the horses tied up so we don't have to catch them again when I get back."

Colleen kept her expression suitably disappointed until his car was out of sight, when she could yell triumphantly, "Yes!" For once, the sheriff's department was helping her plans instead of ruining them.

She and Casey got in another two whole hours together before Mr. Cooke returned. This time he was determined.

"I'm just going to run inside, put my radio on the charger, and grab a couple Pepsis™," he said. "Go ahead and saddle up."

Colleen nodded and turned to Casey. "I guess I have to go now," she said sulkily. "But we should only be gone a little while."

Casey shrugged. "That's okay. I'd go with you, but I think your dad wants me to stay here in case your mom starts having the baby."

Mr. Cooke hurried back out, Andy and Sam following at his heels, tails wagging. They watched expectantly as he shoved two cold Pepsis™ into his saddlebags and mounted his horse, a skittish filly named Snickers. Colleen climbed up on Cammie, the Wonder Slug.

"Ready?" Mr. Cooke said.

"Uh-huh," replied Colleen.

With a practiced movement, Mr. Cooke headed Snickers out of the yard. Sam and Andy immediately darted out in front. Colleen brought up the rear, nearly having to kick Cammie to get her moving. It was going to be a long, boring ride.

To the Top of the Ridge

They struck out away from the houses and angled toward a small trail that led up into the mountains. They usually went up about two or three miles and then turned around. "So," Mr. Cooke said, lounging comfortably in his saddle beside Colleen, "how's it going with Blackie?"

"All right, I guess," Colleen said. She added, "I fed him this morning already."

"Well, that's good. The fatter he gets, the more money you'll make. For the amount of time it takes it's a lot better deal than working a summer job."

"I couldn't get a summer job if I wanted to. I'm only nine."

Mr. Cooke hid a smile. "Oh, yeah, I forgot. You seem like a much older woman." He tugged at a rein, trying to get Snickers to settle down and walk in a straight line. "So what's the latest thing you've decided to be when you grow up?"

"A doctor. Maybe a pediatrician or something."

"A pediatrician? I thought you didn't like babies."

"Well, maybe a horse doctor, then." She glared down at Cammie, taking in the stubborn set of her ears. "If I were a horse doctor, I'd shoot this one. Why can't we get another horse like Dollar?"

"You can ride Snickers as soon as I get her saddle-broke. Right now she's still too jumpy for you to handle."

Colleen looked at the filly doubtfully. "I don't like her, either. I want one like Dollar—fast and pretty."

Mr. Cooke nodded. "He was a good one," he agreed. "I really hated finding him out in the stable like that. But he had a good, long life."

Colleen fell silent for a moment, remembering the day three months before when she had walked in to find her dad sitting alone at the kitchen table. He made her sit down and said quietly, "Colleen, Dollar's dead."

Shocked, she had stumbled out to the stable to find her horse sprawled, unmoving, halfway across the doorway. Her dad hadn't been able to move Dollar's body without help. Colleen had cried for days.

They were approaching the spot in the trail where they usually turned around. Colleen let Cammie slow down—the one thing she was good at. But instead of stopping, her father abruptly cut off onto another trail. Shrugging, Colleen followed. Andy and Sam were already plunging ahead through the underbrush.

The path led up through several shimmering stands of aspens and tall "lodgepole" pines, thin, fragrant trees straight as telephone poles. After about a mile it branched off into a shallow creek—or "crik" as the locals called it. Mr. Cooke and Colleen continued upward for over an hour following the winding creekbed.

Despite her earlier impatience, Colleen was starting to enjoy herself. The creek looked kind of pretty with the weeping willows leaning out over the banks. Their long, dangling leaves danced in the light breeze.

But Snickers was getting increasingly edgy. She kept shying away from the swaying willows, shuddering each time they brushed her face or slid along her flanks. The dogs were also making her nervous by running back and forth. Finally reaching a narrow spot where she would have to squeeze through the willows, Snickers balked.

Mr. Cooke motioned for Colleen to go on ahead. "Maybe she'll do it if you go through first," he said. "She's really acting skittish."

Colleen nodded. Nudging Cammie's ribs, she urged her on. The placid horse clopped through with little protest. Behind her, however, Snickers still stubbornly refused to move. Mr. Cooke sighed.

"Go ahead to the top," he said. "It's not far. I'll meet you up there in a minute."

Colleen picked her way slowly, enjoying the cool mountain air. Small pockets of snow were still scattered here and there in the shade, but the sun was warm and pleasant, the sky a vivid, cloudless blue. *This really wasn't such a bad idea after all*, she thought.

Reaching the top of the ridge, Colleen slid down off Cammie and stood gazing out over the valley. A moment later her father and Snickers showed up. The filly's ears were back, her eyes still rolling with alarm. Colleen grinned.

"I guess you finally talked her into doing it, huh?"

Mr. Cooke got off the horse. "There wasn't much conversation involved," he said dryly. "I'm afraid if I'd started talking back there it might've melted her ears."

"Would've served her right."

Mr. Cooke walked over to stand beside her and take in the view. "See that?" He pointed off to some tiny-looking houses down in the valley. "That's Grandma and Grandpa's ranch. And that whole clump of houses over there is the town of Driggs."

"It looks neat from up here. I've never been this far up before."

"Yep." Mr. Cooke stretched, enjoying himself. "Whew, it's a little warm here in the sun. You ready for a Pepsi?"

"Sure." Colleen settled herself comfortably on a large boulder as her father walked over to rummage in his saddlebags. Sam and Andy were still exploring, crisscrossing the area with their noses to the ground. It was peaceful and beautiful looking out over the valley, like sitting at the top of the world. Colleen wasn't really paying attention when her father started back with the Pepsis, circling around behind Snickers. He had only taken a few steps when he dropped one of the drinks, and he bent automatically to pick it up.

A loud swishing sound made Colleen jerk her head around in alarm. In that frozen instant she noticed two things: Snickers' tail twitching nervously—and her father landing violently on the ground. He rolled over and struggled to his knees, his hands cupped to his face where Snickers had kicked him. Dark blood was gushing out between his fingers.

"Dad!" she gasped, leaping to her feet. Her movement startled Snickers, who swished her tail again and then wheeled to bolt off down the path. Colleen ignored her, running over to drop to her knees beside her father.

Mr. Cooke toppled back weakly into an awkward sitting position, his hands still clamped to his face. His breath was coming in deep, wheezing gasps. He drew his knees to his chest, curling up into a ball, and groaned as blood continued to pour down his hands and onto his yellow sweatshirt. His arms and sleeves were already soaked.

"Dad!" Colleen shrieked. "What's the matter? What happened?"

Mr. Cooke didn't answer. He just rocked back and forth, not seeming to know she was there. Colleen looked around in a panic. What should she do? *I can use his radio to call his deputy,* she thought. Then she remembered that her father had put his radio on the charger just before they left. She was cut off from help.

Just then Andy and Sam ran over. Sensing that something was wrong, they crowded protectively around Mr. Cooke. It gave Colleen an idea. If she could get one of them to go home, maybe she could tie her wind breaker under their collar. That would send a signal to her mom that something was wrong.

She stood up. "Go home, Andy!" she yelled, clapping her hands. "Go home, Sam! Go get help!" If they looked as if they were going to obey, she would call them back long enough to attach her jacket.

Andy whined but stubbornly refused to leave Mr. Cooke's side. Sam retreated a few steps, then slinked back, looking guilty. Neither was going to go.

Colleen looked down at her dad. His jeans as well as his shirt were now covered in blood. She had to do something fast before he bled to death.

"I'm going to get help, Dad," she said, her voice trembling. "Just hang on, okay?" Mr. Cooke didn't respond.

Cammie was waiting patiently, still tired and sweaty from the long climb up the mountainside. Colleen flung herself into the saddle and grabbed the reins. She had to get home fast!

But after she followed the creekbed down several hundred yards, she realized with a sinking heart that she wasn't sure of her way. The creek branched off in several directions. Taking the wrong branch might cost precious time—and perhaps even her father's life. She hesitated, wondering if she should turn back.

Dad needs help, she told herself. *I've got to keep going.*

Still, even as she continued down the mountain, she couldn't shake off a nagging feeling that she should go back to her dad. What if he died while she was gone? She stopped again and sat thinking, chewing her lip. She remembered her father's blood-soaked clothes. In first-aid training in 4-H the year before, she had learned how quickly people could bleed to death. She'd also learned some ways to stop bleeding.

She turned Cammie around. "Come on, girl. We're going back up."

Race Against Time

When Colleen reached the top of the ridge, her dad hadn't moved. He was still huddled on the ground clutching his face, Andy and Sam beside him. Blood was now staining the ground all around him as well as his clothes. Colleen hopped down and ran to him.

"Dad!" she said. She was afraid to touch him. "Dad, I'm back."

She wasn't sure at first that he had heard her, but after a moment he turned his head toward her. When

"You're going to be okay, Dad," she said soothingly. "But you need to get up. We need to keep going." She didn't know what else to do. She realized that if she didn't get him to a doctor soon, he was going to die right in front of her.

After a few minutes Mr. Cooke seemed to get stronger. Colleen helped him stand up again and once again urged him down the trail.

The next few hours were an increasing nightmare for Colleen. As her father weakened, he leaned on her heavier and heavier. He also grew more and more confused. Each time he stumbled and fell Colleen had to nag him until he got up again.

After walking over three hours, they were still only part of the way back down the mountain. Mr. Cooke slumped back to the ground again, almost fainting. Andy and Sam pressed in close to him, whining anxiously, but this time he wouldn't get back up.

"Dad!" Colleen said, tugging gently at his arm. "Come on! I think Mom is having her baby now. We've got to get back home. You don't want to miss that, do you? Mom would be really upset."

At first Mr. Cooke wouldn't listen. But Colleen was determined. "Dad, come *on!*"

Her firm voice seemed to get his attention at last. A moment later he was up and wobbling down the trail again beside her.

But their progress was, if anything, even more slow and halting. Mr. Cooke no longer knew where he was or what was happening. He moved as if he was in a dream. The injury had so affected him, and now only Colleen's hand and voice kept him going.

It took another two hours to reach the foot of the mountain. When Colleen saw the forestry road they'd crossed earlier that day, she sighed with relief. She hadn't led her father down the wrong way after all.

She jumped when she heard a loud crashing sound in the bushes nearby. She whirled around in time to see a dark filly burst out of the brush. It was Snickers!

Although she was glad to have found her father's runaway horse, she was almost disappointed. If only it had run home, her mom would have known that something was wrong. They might've been found hours before.

"Dad, I'm going to ride to the house now to bring back help for you," she said. "I want you to keep walking though, okay?"

Her father's eyes were glazed with pain. "Okay," he murmured.

Colleen hopped up on Cammie. Her father just stood there, swaying.

"Are you going to keep walking?" she asked sharply. He was so weak, so covered with blood. She was afraid that if he sat down he might die.

Her voice snapped him back to attention. "Yes," he said distinctly. As if to show he understood, he took one halting step, then another. Colleen nodded.

"Okay. I'll be right back!"

She gave Cammie a firm kick with both heels. Startled, the horse took off tugging at the reins. This was one time the old slowpoke would have to fly!

"Come on, come on!" Colleen urged, leaning forward in the saddle. "Move it, you stupid horse!" She looked around when she heard pounding hoofbeats behind her. Snickers galloped up alongside her and shot past, heading for home.

Back at the Cookes' house Mrs. Cooke was starting to get worried as she worked outside in the garden. Her husband and daughter usually didn't stay gone this long when they went out riding. She kept glancing up hoping to see them. She was relieved when she finally heard a wild whinny and the sharp thud of hooves. But her eyes widened as Snickers, frightened and soaked with sweat, burst into the yard. She jumped up, her heart pounding.

"Casey!" she shouted, running around to where her young brother-in-law was tinkering with the four-wheeler. "Something's happened to Kim and Colleen! Go see if you can find them!"

Casey nodded as he jumped into the four-wheeler. A moment later he was roaring up the road, heading up the road toward the mountains.

Colleen heard the noisy engine before she spotted Casey. She pulled Cammie to a clopping halt as Casey screeched up beside her.

"Dad's right back there along the road!" she said breathlessly, pointing. "He's hurt really bad!"

"I'll go get him," Casey said. "You go home. I'll catch up with you on the way back."

As Casey roared off in one direction Colleen galloped off in the other. She was still a quarter mile from home when Casey sped past her, heading back home. His older brother's bloody form was sprawled across the four-wheeler's small back seat. Colleen, relieved, drummed her heels against Cammie's ribs, racing along behind them.

At the house, Casey jumped out and quickly helped his brother inside. Mrs. Cooke told him that an ambulance was already on the way.

A moment later Colleen galloped up. Standing outside, she told Casey tearfully what had happened.

"I think Snickers kicked Dad," she sobbed. "His face is all messed up and dented in. I told him to keep walking."

Casey nodded. "He was stumbling along beside the road, kind of in a daze, when I drove up," he reported. "When I got close he yelled, 'Over here!' I tried to get him to wait out here for the ambulance but he wanted to take a bath. I don't think he knows how bad he is."

"I kept telling him the whole time that it wasn't all that bad, that Mom would clean him up when we got home," Colleen said. "I said anything I could think of to keep him going. He kept stopping and not wanting to get back up."

Mr. Cooke's deputy soon arrived with the ambulance close behind. Neighbors, seeing all the commotion, wandered over into the front yard thinking Mrs. Cooke was finally having her baby. They were shocked to learn that the sheriff had been hurt high in the mountains—and that Colleen had single-handedly led him down to safety.

"That was brave of you," the deputy told Colleen. "Your dad's a tough man, but I don't think he'd have made it down if you hadn't been pushing him."

"I just couldn't leave him up there," Colleen said. "Every time I tried, this little voice kept saying, 'Stay with him, don't leave him.'"

"Well, I'm glad you listened. You saved his life."

Mr. Cooke insisted on changing into clean clothes before getting onto the stretcher. But as soon as he was carried out the front door he started vomiting again. The deputy and the EMTs—Emergency Medicial Technicians—quickly loaded him into the ambulance and took off for the hospital, sirens wailing. Mrs. Cooke followed with the deputy.

Colleen and Casey remained behind to take care of the horses. Since Colleen was under twelve she wouldn't be allowed in to see her father at the hospital anyway. After they unsaddled Snickers and Cammie, Colleen went over to her grandparents' house to try to rest. But every time she closed her eyes the horrible image of her father's mangled face rose before her. Would he be okay? Was there something else she should have done? She prayed for him again before she fell asleep.

Her father's injuries were even worse than she'd thought. Almost every bone in the right side of his face was shattered and he couldn't see at all from his right eye. Bone splinters had entered his brain, which was partially exposed along his forehead. It was one of the worst head injuries the doctors had ever seen. They would have to operate to piece back together his face and forehead.

The next morning Colleen's Uncle Brett drove her to the hospital to be with her mom and dad. But despite her pleas, the nurses still wouldn't let her in to see her father. Her grandmother finally cornered one of the nurses.

"Young lady," she snapped. "My granddaughter saved her father's life, and she should be able to go in and see him. Do you understand?" The nurse's mouth dropped open, but she hastily moved out of the way. Soon Colleen was following her grandmother and mother into her father's hospital room.

Her first sight of her father made her gasp. His head was a thick mass of bandages, his right eye was covered and tubes were running into his body from every direction. He looked weak and pale.

But when he heard them come in, his good eye fluttered open. He smiled faintly. "Hi," he murmured, holding out his hand to Colleen.

She stepped close to his bed. "Hi," she said, grasping his large, calloused hand in her small one. "How are you feeling?"

"I'm okay." His voice was quieter than usual. He seemed to study her for a moment before adding, "I love you, Colleen."

Colleen felt a lump rise in her throat. He didn't usually talk like that. "I love you, too, Dad," she said. A few minutes later, when he drifted back off to sleep, he was still holding her hand.

Mr. Cooke went into surgery that night. Doctors carefully removed the bone splinters from his brain, then tried to piece his shattered forehead back together again. Although he couldn't see with his right eye, doctors hoped his sight might return in time.

A Recovered Father and a New Sister

Over the next few days Colleen stayed at the hospital as much as possible. She tried her best to keep her mom cheered up. It was a lot for her mother to deal with, especially with the baby due any minute.

During Mr. Cooke's third night in the hospital Mrs. Cooke went into labor. She checked into the hospital and settled into a room two floors below her husband. Early the next morning she gave birth to a girl.

Colleen had spent the night with other relatives. When she woke up the next morning she learned that she had a baby sister. She jumped up and dressed quickly. A sister! It didn't seem possible.

On the way to the hospital Colleen wondered what the baby would look like. Reaching the nursery window, she peered in through the glass until she found the bassinet labeled "Baby Cooke." A tiny red infant with a patch of dark hair was wrapped in a pink blanket, sound asleep. Colleen stared, then found herself grinning. A little sister!

Colleen went in first to see her mom; then she rode the elevator up to see her dad. Earlier that morning, the nurses had wheeled Mr. Cooke downstairs to meet his new daughter. Because of all the other excitement, the Cookes hadn't decided yet on the baby's name.

Colleen thought that was ridiculous. "You guys can't just not *name* her," she said indignantly when she went back downstairs to see her mom. "What are you gonna do, wait till she's my age? Come on!"

Mrs. Cooke smiled tiredly. "Well, what do you think about 'Jessica'? We'd talked about that name before."

Colleen shrugged. "Sounds okay to me."

"Why don't you go up and ask your dad what he thinks?" Mrs. Cooke suggested.

"Okay. I'll be right back."

Colleen trotted down the hall to the elevator, pushed the "3," and waited as the elevator rose. Then she got off and went to her father's room.

"Dad," she said as soon as she walked in. "We're trying to name the baby, and Mom wants to know what you think about 'Jessica.'"

Mr. Cooke was sitting up in his bed, propped against pillows. "Jessica? I don't know . . . seems like everybody's naming their daughters Jessica."

Colleen rolled her eyes. "Well, then, what do *you* want to name her? You can't call her 'Baby Cooke' forever, you know."

"I'd kind of like a short name—something that'll be easier when I have to yell for her. How about 'Chuck?'"

"Dad!" Colleen was scandalized. "You can't name *my* little sister 'Chuck'! That's a boy's name."

Mr. Cooke shrugged. "I think it's a great name. Chuck. It's perfect."

Colleen felt dazed. "I can't believe this. I'll go tell Mom. You stay right here."

She went back down the elevator and snaked through the hall to her mother's room again. But when she walked in, she got a surprise. The nurse was just bringing in her little sister to be fed!

Mrs. Cooke motioned for her to come over to the bed. "Colleen, I'd like you to meet your new sister, Baby Whoever-she-is. Did your father like 'Jessica'?"

Colleen's eyes were glued to the tiny, wriggling baby in her mother's arms. *How could a real human being be so small?* she wondered.

"No. He said everybody's naming kids Jessica. He wants to name her 'Chuck.'"

"Chuck?" Mrs. Cooke laughed. "No, I don't think so. She definitely doesn't look like a Chuck."

Colleen was stroking the baby's tiny arm. "Can I hold her?"

"If you'll sit right here next to me. You just have to be careful to hold her neck. It flops around."

Colleen edged onto the bed and her mother settled the baby into her arms. She was so small and light that it was like holding a box of tissues.

"Hi, Baby," Colleen said softly. "I'm your big sister, did you know that?" The baby's eyes opened for a moment and Colleen smiled. "Hey, she's pretty cute!"

"Yep," Mrs. Cooke said. "But you need to give her back now so I can feed her. Go tell Dad that no daughter of mine is going to be named 'Chuck', and ask what he thinks about 'Kimberly.'"

Colleen sighed. "I can't believe you guys. Did you do this when I was born?"

"We picked your name months before you were born. We just didn't get around to it this time."

It took another three trips up and down the elevator before both parents agreed on a name: Cassie Dawn Cooke. Exhausted, Colleen sat on the bed beside her mother and little sister.

"Well, Cassie," she said, stroking the baby's arm. "Good thing I was here to make sure you got a good name. Otherwise you'd have been stuck with Chuck."

A few days later, when Mrs. Cooke took Cassie home from the hospital, Mr. Cooke had to stay behind. When his vision still hadn't returned after ten days, the doctors decided to operate again. This time they removed his damaged right eye.

It was upsetting, but Mr. Cooke didn't let it get him down. "Losing an eye is better than dying," he said. "If it hadn't been for Colleen I would've died for sure."

Colleen received two local awards for "courage in the face of adversity" and "a heroic act to save a human life." That fall she was also chosen as one of ten "young heroes" across the nation. She and her parents were flown to Washington, D.C., for an awards ceremony, where Colleen was photographed with then President Ronald Reagan. He sent her the picture, signed: "To Colleen Cooke, a real American hero."

Mr. Cooke eventually went back to work at the sheriff's department, sporting a black eye patch that he claimed made him look "dashing." And despite the near-tragedy on their last horse ride, by August he and Colleen were riding together again exploring the hills and ridges around their house.

"So," Mr. Cooke said one bright Saturday afternoon as he and Colleen rode side by side, "I bet you're about ready to go back to school for once, aren't you? This summer has been a little wild."

Colleen tilted her head, thinking. *Yeah, it's been different. You getting hurt, Cassie being born, and now having to sell Blackie. . . .* She looked over at her father and said, "I never thought I could get so attached to that stupid steer. But now every time I walk up, he runs over to be petted. It's really going to be hard to see him go."

Mr. Cooke nodded. "It's tough," he agreed. "But then *you're* tough, too." He grinned. "My daughter, the hero. Guess I'll have to make sure to take you along every time I go out riding from now on, just in case."

Colleen's eyes twinkled. "Maybe you'd better," she said. "You probably need someone more mature to look after you. So until Cassie gets old enough to help out, I guess I'll be stuck with the job."

Colleen at the White House with her parents and the Young Hero award she received from then president Ronald Reagan.

Photo courtesy of *Omaha World-Herald* and Dave Hendee

Blizzard in Wildcat Hills

The Matt Meyers Story

Two pairs of eyes followed Matt Meyers' hand as he trailed a nacho chip dripping with cheese to his mouth and crunched it loudly. The muscular fifteen-year-old was sitting at his bedroom desk snacking as he flipped through the newest issue of *Outdoor Life*. Katie and Sadie, the household pets, sat at his knee watching as his plate of nachos slowly dwindled. It was a quiet Sunday afternoon in March 1992.

Katie, a springer spaniel with long brown ears, licked her lips and looked mournful; Sadie, a pure white cat, fixed her ice blue eyes on Matt without blinking. It was clear that they were both sending the same urgent message: *Feed me.*

Matt finally closed the magazine. "Okay, okay!" he laughed, patting Katie's head and tickling the cat's chin. "Lucky for you guys I made enough to share." Breaking off one last chip for himself, he put the plate down on the floor. Katie and Sadie both loved nachos.

Matt went to the window and peered out. Although most of Nebraska was plains country, the Meyers' house was nestled near the bottom of a canyon in the Wildcat Hills, part of the North Platte Valley. The back of the house overlooked the densely wooded canyon, while Matt's window faced the rolling hillside. Today, the slice of sky visible over the pine trees in the yard was clear. Matt looked down at Katie. "Hey, girl, want to go for a walk?"

The springer spaniel's ears perked up. Tail wagging, she ran to the door and pressed her nose to the crack, snuffling loudly. Matt paused only long enough to grab his parka and pull on his new buckskin-colored cowboy hat, straightening the brim to a manly angle.

Mrs. Meyers smiled when Matt stopped by the kitchen on his way out to tell her where he was going.

"I don't suppose you picked up your dirty clothes so I could wash them, did you?" she asked. Matt shook his head, and she sighed. "You know, I keep hoping that someday you'll get tired of living in a pigpen. Doesn't it ever bother you?"

Matt grinned. "I like my room just the way it is," he said. "And I sure hope you're not thinking about getting into one of your cleaning moods today. I hate walking in and finding everything rearranged—and I *really* hate those ruffly little white things you keep hanging on my windows!"

Mrs. Meyers looked innocent. "I think they're called 'curtains,'" she said helpfully.

"What do I need curtains for? There's nobody out here to look inside anyway."

Mrs. Meyers rolled her eyes. "Weren't you," she asked pointedly, "going on a walk?"

"Okay, okay, I'm leaving. Just stay out of my room—please."

"I'll think about it," his mom smiled.

"Think hard." He leaned over to plant a quick kiss on her cheek. "And remember, *no ruffles.*"

Katie raced outside ahead of him, ready as always for adventure. The air was cold, but not bitter—a perfect day for exploring. "Come on, Katie," he said. "Let's go check out the canyon."

Matt had always been the outdoorsman among the Meyers' three sons. Mike, eighteen, liked to hunt and fish, but was hardly ever home; Andy, eleven, liked bow-hunting, but he usually spent most of his time playing Nintendo™ or listening to music. Matt was the one who liked getting out and doing active things

whether it was fishing, playing football with the Gering High Bulldogs, or working out at the school gym.
It drove him crazy to just sit around.

Ducking under the barbed-wire fence, Matt and
Katie cut across the pasture where Comanche and
Marco, the family's two horses, grazed happily. Then
they started down the slope into the canyon. Matt had
discovered a lot of interesting things there: eagles'
nests, coyote bones, even a rattlesnake or two. He had
a small collection of stuff on top of his dresser.

This time, however, he saw nothing worth keeping.
He started back home, wondering if he could talk his
mom into driving him into town to see a movie or
something. His girlfriend, Andrea, might be able to
meet him there. Since she was sixteen, she could
already drive.

But that plan, too, was shot down when his mother
said she couldn't take him. Disappointed, Matt wandered into the living room where Andy sat glued as
usual to the Nintendo.™ Matt plopped down on the
floor beside him and grabbed the other controller. "Let
me play you," he said, punching the reset button.

"Hey!" Andy squawked, his freckles standing out
on his flushed face. "I was in the middle of a game!
You can't just come in here like that and—"

"Too late," Matt said with a smirk as he loaded Super
Mario Brothers.™ "You want to play or not?"

"I guess so. But I'm gonna beat you."

"In your dreams, little brother."

But by the time they got to the eighth world, Matt was hopelessly behind, with only one life left. Andy had thirty. Exasperated, Matt threw down the controller and stood up.

"You can have your stupid game back. This is too boring."

Andy looked smug. "It's not boring when you know how to play."

"Fine, Nintendo™ Master. Rot your tiny little brain and see if I—"

"Matthew!" Mrs. Meyers had walked unseen into the living room. "Stop it. And you too, Andrew!" It was always a bad sign when she started using their full names. "All you two do is argue over that stupid Nintendo. One of these days I'm going to toss it right off the deck and down into the canyon."

"It wasn't me!" Andy protested. "Matt came in here and—"

"I don't care. Just *get along,* will you?"

Disgusted, Matt retreated to his room. *Why couldn't he have been an only child?* he wondered. He kicked irritably at a pile of dirty clothes and glanced around his room. Fishing poles were scattered across his floor. Clothes were hanging out of most of his drawers. His bed wasn't made. A jumble of shoes—track shoes, football cleats, boots, tennis shoes—were spilling out of his closet, most of them stuffed with dirty socks. Matt sniffed the air and made a face. The place really *was* a pigpen!

He turned to Katie, who was watching him with her head cocked to one side. "Guess it's time to clean up in here, huh, girl?" he said, his good humor returning. "Maybe we can keep Mom from having another ruffle attack."

The next morning, back in school, Matt greeted Gabe and B. J., both on the football team with him. He was glad to learn there'd be a substitute that day in English class.

"That's good," he said. "All this Greek and Roman mythology stuff lately is getting me down. I'd rather run ten miles than memorize another 'Ode to Flepidious' or whatever. I'm not into poems written by fat old men in dresses." Gabe and B. J. quickly agreed.

The English substitute turned out to be a big, grim-looking woman. She announced that they'd be watching a filmstrip about ancient Rome. Matt settled back in his chair, considering a nap. But as soon as the lights went out, he realized that the projector beam was shining directly over his head. It gave him an idea.

He glanced at the teacher. She had her back turned, looking over some papers. Meshing his fingers together, Matt slipped his hands up into the light, casting a dog-shaped shadow onto the screen. It appeared to be surfing blissfully down the Nile River. The class broke up with laughter.

The teacher whirled around, but by then Matt was sitting innocently at his desk, his hands in his lap. She eyed them all suspiciously and then turned back to her papers. Matt waited a moment and did it again, this time accompanying the dog's journey down the Nile with a soft howling sound.

The teacher spun around, her pudgy face quivering. "All right!" she snapped. "I don't know what's so funny but you'd all better pay attention. No more monkey business."

Undaunted, Matt managed to fit in one more "dog show" before the film ended. Too bad they couldn't have a substitute every day!

He was walking down the hall when his best friend, Jason Rounds, spotted him.

"Matt!" Jason called, running to catch up. "Are you staying after school today to work out?"

Matt shrugged. "I guess so. I might lift weights for a while."

"Good. Me too."

Jason, an inch shorter than Matt but just as muscular, was also on the football team. The two teenagers had spent many weekends hiking and camping in the Wildcat Hills, and they were both looking forward to getting their driver's licenses in a few more months. No more begging their parents or friends for rides every time they wanted to go someplace, or worse yet, having to be driven on dates. Freedom!

"You feel like doing some hunting this weekend?" Matt asked.

Jason shook his head ruefully. "I wish I could, but my mom has a bunch of stuff she wants me to do around the house. She'll have a fit if I even ask. Maybe next weekend, okay?"

"Okay. I'll meet you in the gym after school."

On the way to his next class, Matt reflected that that was the only bad thing about living in the middle of nowhere—being isolated from friends. Still, given the choice, he wouldn't trade places with anybody. In the three years since his family had moved away from town he'd grown to love the freedom of being able to wander, either on foot or on horseback, through the rugged hills and canyons. It was worth the inconvenience and occasional loneliness.

As it turned out, that weekend was damp and gloomy. Matt moped around the house Saturday morning, then talked his dad into going riding with him. They saddled up Comanche and Marco and trotted off into the rolling hills.

Mr. Meyers' thinning hair blew in the breeze as he rode beside Matt, talking quietly about a difficult case he was handling at work. His job as a criminal probation officer required him to deal constantly with the darker side of human nature—one reason he enjoyed coming home every day to peaceful surroundings. Matt listened, secretly proud of his father's toughness and resolve. Any criminal who thought he could mess around with him would be in for a surprise!

The sky had that cold, heavy look that might mean snow later on. When it started to drizzle, they turned back. Winter storms in Nebraska could be brutal.

The Adventure Begins

The dreary weather lasted the rest of the afternoon and into the next day. Matt spent Sunday morning helping his dad take apart the washing machine to remove a shoestring—Andy's, of course—that had been sucked into the pump. By the time they were finished, Matt was feeling restless. Gloomy skies or not, he needed to get out of the house!

"I'm going out to split some wood," he told his dad at around two o'clock. "Then I think I'll mess around for a while at the shooting range." The state highway patrol's small shooting range, usually deserted on weekends, was about a quarter of a mile away.

Mr. Meyers nodded. "I'd go with you but I think your mother has some chores planned for me."

"I probably won't stay long anyway. It looks as if it might rain again, and I don't want to ruin my hat." He was wearing the new buckskin-colored hat, the brim pulled low over his forehead. It had already become his favorite.

"Don't forget that your mother's cooking a big dinner tonight," Mr. Meyers warned. "She'll be upset if you're late."

"Are you kidding? Me miss a meal?" Grinning, Matt headed outside, Katie at his heels. The springer spaniel had always had the uncanny ability to appear the instant anybody whispered "walk" or "outside." Matt had decided long ago that she must have better hearing than Superman.

The Meyers kept their firewood stacked on a wooden pallet at the side of the house, most of it in big logs that needed to be split. Matt hefted the heavy axe with a sigh. It might not be exciting, but it would be good exercise. And after two days of hanging around the house he certainly needed it!

Katie watched from a safe distance as Matt swung the axe steadily, sending wood chips flying. He split a large pile of wood, then stacked it neatly on the pallet, ready for use. It should be enough to keep the fireplace going for the next week anyway.

The minute he put the axe away Katie jumped up, her eyes bright. "Okay, girl," he said, brushing the sawdust off his jeans. "We can go now."

They walked briskly across the pasture and ducked under the barbed-wire fence that marked the edge of their property. The shooting range was hidden by a small clump of trees in the distance.

Ten minutes later they reached the range. It wasn't much; just four wooden posts where people could stand while they shot into the steep dirt bank. Matt picked up a stick and started digging in the loose dirt, looking for shells. He'd found some really interesting ones in the past, mushroomed out in all kinds of odd shapes. He liked to take the best ones home.

He unearthed about ten or fifteen and dropped them into his jacket pockets. A few appeared to be brand new. Then he made a real find: a perfect brass-colored tip and a matching silver casing. He slid them together to make what looked like a real bullet. That one would look great on his dresser!

He was still digging around when a sharp gust of unexpectedly cold air hit the back of his neck. He looked up, startled to discover that a dense fog had swept in all around him. It was so thick that he could no longer see the wooden poles just twenty feet away.

"Katie!" he said, his voice sounding strangely muffled, "come on. We have to go."

The brown-and-white spaniel trotted out of the fog, her fur glistening with moisture. The temperature felt like it had dropped twenty degrees in just seconds. Matt stood still for a moment, trying to get his bearings. It was a little unnerving not to be able to see the familiar landmarks that pointed toward home.

Still, he was only ten minutes from the house. How difficult could it be? He struck out through the cold, damp fog, walking slowly to keep from straying off course. The wind picked up and rain started falling around him in fat, cold drops. He pulled his hat lower and tried to hurry. Where was the stupid barbed-wire fence, anyway? It seemed like he'd been walking a lot longer than ten minutes. He wished he'd worn his watch.

Then he spotted it just ahead through the fog. More relieved than he liked to admit, he hurried forward. Under the fence, across the pasture and he'd be home, he told himself. It would feel good to thaw out in front of the fireplace. His face and feet were freezing.

It wasn't until he put his hand on the top strand of wire that he realized something was wrong. He stared in disbelief at the rusty barbed wire and grey, weathered fence posts. His family's fence was almost new.

I must've gone the wrong way, he thought with a sinking heart. He knew that a few distant neighbors lived to the north and west of his house, but he was sure he'd never seen this particular fence before. The rest of the area was wilderness. Where *was* he?

The rain was rapidly changing to an icy mixture of sleet and snow. Matt pulled a pair of thin gloves out of his parka and put them on. What should he do now?

Maybe there's a house somewhere around here, he thought. *If so I could get directions.*

"Hey!" he yelled. "Anybody here?"

Nothing. He tried again.

"Help!"

Still nothing. When Katie whined, he turned around with a sigh. Leaning into the stinging wind, he started back the way they'd come. At least, he *thought* it was the way they'd come; in the dense, clinging fog it was hard to tell for sure. But after he'd walked for what seemed like thirty minutes without finding the shooting range, Matt realized he'd gotten his directions confused again.

The sky was growing steadily darker; the wind, more violent. He clenched his teeth, trying to stop his shivering. This was crazy. He *had* to get home soon.

His mom and dad would be mad, thinking he was just out fooling around.

Then he spotted a weathered log fence through the fog that looked familiar. He knew this place! It was a small corral he'd seen a few times in the distance, about a mile southeast of his house. Surely he could find his way back from here.

Peering through the blowing snow and fog, trying to get his directions straight, he gradually picked out a dark shape nestled back among the trees off to one side. It was a cabin!

"Come on, Katie!" he said, hurrying forward with relief. He pictured the welcome blast of warm air as the people inside opened the door. It would be embarrassing to explain how he'd gotten turned around in the fog, but he was too frozen to worry about it. He'd call Dad and get him to pick them up. Now that safety was near he could admit to himself that he wasn't really sure he could find his way home anymore. The snowfall was fast becoming a blizzard.

But when he ran up the steps to the cabin, he saw that there was a giant padlock on the door. He hesitated, then knocked. There was no answer.

"Anybody home?" he yelled, banging harder. He finally walked around to look in the window. The dusty, deserted look told him nobody had lived there for a while.

Matt glanced back out at the swirling fog and snow, feeling sick—and for the first time, a little afraid. He was tempted to break one of the windows and climb inside, out of the biting wind. He could build a fire, and he and Katie could thaw out and wait for the storm to blow over.

But he could just picture his dad's reaction if he found out he'd broken into somebody house: "You did *what?*" Reluctantly, he trudged back down the steps. He'd have to walk home after all.

Using the corral as a reference point, he aimed himself in the direction where his house should be. All he had to do was go straight. He tried not to think about how difficult that had already proved to be.

He had hiked briskly for about fifteen minutes in what felt like an arrow-straight line when he spotted footprints in the snow just ahead. It took him a moment to realize they were his and Katie's. He stopped, the shock leaving him panicked and dangerously near tears. They had walked in a circle!

He was still fighting for control when Katie took off without warning, leaving him standing there. She was instantly swallowed up by the fog.

"Katie!" Matt screamed. "Don't you leave me here!" Charging after her, he spotted her darting along past a tree. He tackled her and pinned her to the ground before bursting into tears.

"You stupid dog!" he said hysterically. "Don't you take off like that! You're all I've got."

Katie seemed to understand his words. She licked his face apologetically, and when he loosened his hold she didn't try to squirm away. Matt sat up and buried his face in her damp fur. *Fifteen-year-olds,* he told himself, *didn't just go out for walks and die.* When he got home he'd probably laugh about all this.

If he got home, a small voice mocked. He pushed the thought away. Things like that happened to other people, strangers in the newspapers. No way would something like that happen to him!

The wind was howling, with the snow falling heavier every minute. Shivering, he pulled his parka closer, wishing he'd worn heavier clothes. What time was it—six o'clock? Seven? The thought made him realize how hungry he was.

He wished he had some way to get a message to his mom, to let her know he was sorry about ruining her big dinner. Would she know he was trying his best to get back home?

Then he remembered a cherry cough drop he'd stuck in his jeans pocket. He fished it out clumsily with his half-frozen fingers and bit it in half, giving a piece to Katie and popping the other half in his mouth. The tingling menthol taste soothed and warmed his throat as he sucked on it gratefully. It wasn't much, but it was better than nothing.

Darkness was rapidly descending, and the storm still showed no signs of letting up. Matt started off again, his feet feeling like huge blocks of ice. His shivering increased as he hiked across a pasture, then into a small stand of trees. A sign was nailed to one of them, barely readable in the deep gloom: "State Land—No Hunting."

Matt stared in dismay. He'd combed the hills for miles around his house, but he'd never seen that sign before in his life. Wherever he was, it was nowhere near home. Slowly, like an automaton, he turned and started off again.

This is impossible, he thought numbly. *I have no idea where I am. How am I supposed to find my way home?*

Still, what choice do I have? He forged on, stumbling up hills and through deepening snow drifts. Dampness seeped into his hair and clothes. His stomach became a hard knot from shivering. Hours passed; but in his state of mind, time no longer had meaning. Nothing he saw looked even vaguely familiar.

He was trudging blindly down a steep hill when he lost his footing. With a startled shout he skidded down the slope and splashed feet-first in a shallow water hole. The shock of the icy water took his breath away. It seeped into his leather boots, soaking his socks and jeans legs. He was still gasping when Katie plunged in beside him and began to drink thirstily.

"Katie, *no!*" he shouted in a panic. Grabbing her collar, he dragged her roughly out of the water. The cold was deadly enough without getting wet. He could already feel the numbing effects on his own body. The wind hitting his wet jeans felt like a knife.

Hauling the dog with him, Matt struggled back up the slope and struck off in a different direction. His eyes burned from the cold and his legs felt like lead. His movements became increasingly slow and jerky. Each step took an effort.

It must be almost midnight, he decided. Maybe if he could rest for a few minutes he would feel stronger. Spotting a pine tree with low spreading branches, he veered over and crawled under it. Katie crawled in after him and leaned against him, resting her head on his chest so he could stroke her ears.

But somehow, despite his exhaustion, Matt couldn't relax. The shelter of the tree felt wrong, not *safe*, somehow. Katie whined and nudged him, seeming to feel the same way. It didn't make sense, Matt thought tiredly, but maybe God was trying to tell them something. If so, they'd better listen. He crawled back out and stood up, swaying with weakness. He was shivering so hard that his teeth were banging together.

In the dark, howling confusion of wind and snow there was no way to even guess at directions. Matt stumbled along aimlessly until he came to another stand of trees. One, a spruce, had thick branches that drooped all the way down to the ground, kind of like a tent. Hardly aware of what he was doing, Matt dropped to his knees and crawled under it. He leaned back against the tree trunk, miserable and nearly delirious. This was a nightmare.

Katie whined and pressed close to him, shivering. Slowly, painfully, Matt uncurled his cold-numbed fingers and unzipped his jacket to stretch it around her.

Even though it was damp, it would help shield her from the wind.

Lost in the Snowstorm

The storm continued to rage, blowing snow in on top of them. Matt closed his eyes and let his mind drift. What if he ended up dying out here? There were so many things he'd planned to do: get his driver's license . . . start high school next year . . . someday even get married. Why would God want to take him now? His mom and dad would be so upset.

The thought of his parents stopped him. Did they even realize that he was in trouble? Or did they think he'd just gotten mad about something and stormed off? He wished there was some way to tell them what had happened and how much he loved them.

Please, God, he prayed in a daze. *Let them understand. And even if I have to die out here, please take care of Katie. It's not her fault I got her into this.*

He woke up abruptly some time later. Confused, thinking he was at home, he sprang up—and banged his head on a branch. Then he remembered where he was. The cold hit him anew with a pain that ripped from his head to his toes, leaving his whole body shaking in uncontrollable spasms. He started to cry.

"I can't take this!" he sobbed through frozen lips. "God, why'd this happen to me? Either take me now or get me out of here!"

Sinking back to the ground, he continued to sob hysterically. He'd never felt so alone in his life. Why had this happened to him? What had he done to deserve it?

Eventually he fell back into a fitful sleep. After a few minutes he was shivering so hard that his arms and legs flopped around by themselves, slamming against the frozen ground. He kept waking up feeling as if he was being shaken. He had no sensation anymore in his legs or feet. Unable to control his bladder, he wet his pants. It no longer seemed to matter.

Once, in a delirium, he prayed again. If he was getting ready to meet God, he thought he'd better get some things straight.

"I'm sorry I yelled at you before," he mumbled. "And I'm sorry I've treated Andy so bad. If you take me back home I'll try to be nicer to him." He swallowed painfully. "Please, I just want to go home!"

When he next opened his eyes, dim light was filtering down through the tree branches. Matt stared up in a daze. It was morning!

"Katie . . . ?" he said groggily. A thin powder of snow had covered him during the night. But at his feet, where Katie had been sleeping, there was now only a large, silent mound of snow. Matt stared in horror, then gently nudged the mound with one of his boots. If Katie was under it, frozen and dead—

But at that moment a lively brown-and-white form came crashing back in through the branches. Matt threw his arms around Katie, almost crying with relief as she whined and licked his face.

A few minutes later, after eating a handful of snow to ease his dry mouth, Matt tried to stand up. His frozen legs collapsed under him. He massaged them and flexed them with his hands, but they still wouldn't hold him. He finally grabbed the tree trunk and pulled himself up inch by inch, hoping he could get his blood circulating again.

As soon as he straightened, however, he was hit with a violent wave of nausea. Sick and dizzy, he leaned against the tree trunk. It was at that moment he heard the faint sound of a plane overhead.

Get out in the open.

The thought drove him to try frantically one more time to walk on legs that felt like dead stumps, but it was no use. He finally dropped back to the ground and tried to roll out from under the branches.

By the time he made it, however, the plane was already gone. He stared up at the empty sky, almost too far gone to care. The snow had stopped, although it was still gloomy and overcast. If he could just get to where he could walk again he would have at least a slim chance of finding his way home. For Katie's sake he had to try.

It took another hour for his legs to grow strong enough to support him. Dragging his cold-deadened feet over the uneven ground, Matt started off down the hill at a slow, stumbling gait. Every movement took an effort. Katie followed as he trudged past a canyon and through several thick stands of trees. They saw a small windmill across a bluff, but nothing Matt recognized as a landmark.

Finally, too weak to go on, he collapsed in the snow. Barely conscious, he curled his knees to his chest as fresh spasms wracked his body. Katie whined and nudged him, urging him to get up, but he ignored her. She finally started digging at his arm with her claws.

"Leave me alone," Matt mumbled miserably. But instead of retreating, Katie shoved her cold, wet nose into his face and let go with a strange, ear-splitting howl. The sound, almost a scream, startled Matt out of his groggy stupor.

"O-okay," he stammered. "I'll get up."

He hauled himself up and forced himself to take one shaky step, then another. He stumbled and fell every few minutes, but Katie howled in his face each time until he got up. She wouldn't let him stop, not even to rest.

The sun was high in the sky, the clouds clearing, as they approached a deep, snow-filled gully. By then Matt was reeling and stumbling like a drunk, his legs crossing each other. No longer able to think or see clearly, he seemed to be moving in slow motion as Katie anxiously pushed him along.

But in the end, Matt's strength just gave out. Faltering, he pitched forward into the snow and lay there weakly, unable to move. *I'm sorry, Mom,* he thought as swirling, icy darkness closed in all around him. *I tried to get home. I tried. . . .*

This time, despite all Katie's frantic efforts, Matt remained motionless, sprawled on the hard, frozen ground.

Search in the Storm

Back at the Meyers' house, panic had set in within hours of Matt's disappearance. It wasn't like him to be late, especially when he knew they'd planned a big family dinner. What's more, a violent snow storm was sweeping into the area. When Matt hadn't returned by four o'clock, they knew something was wrong.

"I'm riding out to look for him," Mr. Meyers said. "If he shows up here, tell him to stay put." Saddling Comanche, he rode over to the shooting range first. The area was thick with fog and snow flurries. There were no footprints, but Matt might have left before it started snowing.

"Matt!" Mr. Meyers called. "Can you hear me?"

He listened, thinking helplessly of the rugged hills and canyons that stretched for miles in every direction. If Matt had gotten lost in the fog, there was no telling where he might have ended up.

At six o'clock they called the sheriff's office. An official search was launched. Over one hundred people turned up to ride and hike through the Wildcat Hills to look for Matt.

But by midnight, with the snow storm raging and the wind-chill factor down to minus-ten degrees, the sheriff had to call everybody back in. He couldn't risk other people's lives in the rescue effort. They would have to wait until the storm died down.

The search couldn't start again until six o'clock the next morning. The hours passed, still with no sign of Matt. When the skies finally cleared around noon, search planes were brought out. Pilots Mark Sinner and Jim Phillips crisscrossed the area for about an hour before they spotted some footprints in the snow. They followed them to Matt.

The ninth grader was sprawled face down in the snow about three miles from his house, a brown and white dog by his side. As they circled overhead the dog barked wildly, but Matt never moved. "Looks like he might not have made it," Mr. Sinner said grimly as he picked up the radio to call in the boy's location.

Mr. Phillips nodded. "Tell them to make sure the mother doesn't go along with the ground crew that comes to pick him up. If it's a body, she doesn't need to remember her son like that."

Matt was being shaken again, but this time somebody was yelling his name. "Matt! Matthew Meyers! Can you hear us?"

Opening his eyes to a slit, Matt saw a confusing blur of faces. Voices were shouting, but nothing they said made sense. He moved his lips with difficulty.

"Ka-Katie," he whispered. "Where's Katie?"

"What did he say?"

"I don't know. I couldn't understand him."

Hands were lifting him, moving him somewhere. Matt caught a brief glimpse of lights along the top of a white van as he was slid inside, then a door slammed.

"Katie . . ."

"Katie?" Suddenly, it was his mother's voice. "Katie's just fine," she said. "She's at home sleeping in front of the fireplace."

Bewildered, Matt opened his eyes. He was in a hospital emergency room. His mom and dad were both there sitting beside his bed.

"Hi," he said hoarsely.

His mother smoothed his hair back from his forehead. "How are you feeling?"

Matt had to think about it. "Okay, I guess. My feet hurt."

"I'm not surprised," his dad said. "They were so swollen the paramedics had to cut your boots off. The pilots who spotted you thought you were dead. You had a really close call, son."

"I know."

Mrs. Meyers continued to stroke his head. "Is there anything we can get for you, honey? You're going to have to stay in the hospital for a while, you know."

Matt thought and a faint glint slowly crept in his red-rimmed eyes. "How about some Skittles™?"

"Candy!" Mrs. Meyers laughed. "I think we can manage that."

Matt fell silent for a moment. "Where's Andy?" he finally asked. "Is he here?" Mr. Meyers nodded. "He's out in the waiting room with Mike. He'll be coming in to see you as soon as you're settled in your room."

"Good." When his parents exchanged a surprised look, Matt managed a weak smile. "I made some promises to God out there," he explained, "that I need to get started on."

Matt suffered from hypothermia and severe frostbite in his feet, but none of his toes had to be cut off. The doctors said his feet would be swollen for a few weeks, but they'd eventually shrink back to normal.

His second day in the hospital, Mr. and Mrs. Meyers brought him a surprise: a new cowboy hat with a giant bag of Skittles inside. His other hat had been reduced to a limp, sodden rag. He tried on the new one with a grin. It fit just right.

To everyone's amazement, Matt was feeling good enough to be released from the hospital by the third day. On the way home he asked his parents if they could stop by his school. Jason, Gabe, and some others had planned to visit him that afternoon and he wanted to tell them he wouldn't be at the hospital.

They arrived at Gering High a half-hour before school let out. Matt hobbled back to his last-period art class, which he shared with Jason Rounds. When he walked in, grinning, the class exploded with excitement. Everybody ran over to hug him, even the teacher. He felt like a celebrity.

After the bell rang, the class surged out into the hall laughing and talking. A moment later, to Matt's surprise, Gabe's mom appeared carrying a big paper bag. Everyone gathered around to watch as she handed it to Matt. It too was packed to the top with Skittles! Gabe explained, "We heard you'd been craving candy. But we got you something else, too. It's in there."

Curious, Matt dug down into the bag until he felt something hard. He pulled it out and laughed. It was a small plastic compass with an attached thermometer!

"Thanks," he said sheepishly. "I guess I need this."

Jason patted his shoulder. "Yeah, well," he said, "next time you go for a walk, just take it with you. There are lots easier ways to get Skittles than this, you know!"

Do You Have a Real Kids, Real Adventures Story?

We're looking for TRUE stories for future volumes of *Real Kids, Real Adventures*—stories about real kids ages nine to seventeen who have faced danger or crisis with extraordinary courage or sometimes become real-life heroes. If you have heard about such a story, we might like to use it. The first person to submit a story that we use will have his or her name mentioned in the book and will receive a free copy of that book when it is published.

Please send your story ideas to: Real Kids, Real Adventures, P.O. Box 461572, Garland, TX 75046-1572. Please include your name, address, phone number with area code, and a newspaper clipping with the name and date of the paper, and/or factual information we can use to research the story.